# Blues
## *for* Mister
## Charlie

*by James Baldwin*

# BLUES
## *for* MISTER
## CHARLIE

*a play by*

## JAMES BALDWIN

*Dial Press · New York · 1964*

Copyright © 1964 by James Baldwin
All rights reserved
Library of Congress catalog card number: 64–15223

Designed by Bernard Brussel-Smith
Manufactured in the United States of America

*To the memory of*
MEDGAR EVERS,
*and his widow and his children,*
*and*
*to the memory of the dead children of Birmingham.*

# BLUES
## *for* MISTER
## CHARLIE

*notes for*
# BLUES

THIS PLAY HAS BEEN on my mind—has been bugging me—for several years. It is unlike anything else I've ever attempted in that I remember vividly the first time it occurred to me; for in fact, it did not occur to me, but to Elia Kazan. Kazan asked me at the end of 1958 if I would be interested in working in the Theatre. It was a generous offer, but I did not react with great enthusiasm because I did not then, and don't now, have much respect for what goes on in the American Theatre. I am not convinced that it *is* a Theatre; it seems to me a series, merely, of commercial speculations, stale, repetitious, and timid. I certainly didn't see much future for me in that frame-work, and I was profoundly unwilling to risk my morale and my talent—my life—in endeavors which could only increase a level of frustration already dangerously high.

Nevertheless, the germ of the play persisted. It is based, very distantly indeed, on the case of Emmett Till—the Negro youth who was murdered in Mississippi in 1955. The murderer in this case was acquitted. (His brother, who helped him do the deed, is now a deputy sheriff in Rulesville, Mississippi.) After his acquittal, he recounted the facts of the murder—for one cannot refer to his performance as a confession—to William Bradford Huie, who wrote it all down in an article called "Wolf Whistle." I do not know why the case pressed on my mind so hard—but it would not let me go. I absolutely dreaded committing myself to writing a play—there were enough people around already telling me that I couldn't write novels—but I began to see that my fear of the form masked a much deeper fear. That fear was that I would never be able to draw a valid portrait of the murderer. In life, obviously, such people baffle and terrify me and, with one part of my mind at least, I hate them and would be willing to kill them. Yet, with another part of my mind, I am aware that no man is a villain in his own eyes. Something in the man knows—*must* know—that what he is doing is evil; but in order to accept the knowledge the man would have to change. What is ghastly and really almost hopeless in our racial situation now is that the crimes we have committed are so great and so unspeakable that the acceptance of this knowledge would lead, literally, to madness. The human being, then, in order to protect himself, closes his eyes, compulsively repeats his crimes, and enters a spiritual darkness which no one can describe.

But if it is true, and I believe it is, that all men are brothers,· then we have the duty to try to understand this wretched man; and while we probably cannot hope to liberate him, begin working toward the liberation of his children. For we, the American people, have created him, he is our servant; it is we who put the cattle-prodder in his hands, and we are responsible for the crimes that he commits. It is we who have locked him in the prison of his color.

It is we who have persuaded him that Negroes are worthless human beings, and that it is his sacred duty, as a white man, to protect the honor and purity of his tribe. It is we who have forbidden him, on pain of exclusion from the tribe, to accept his beginnings, when he and black people loved each other, and rejoice in them, and use them; it is we who have made it mandatory—honorable—that white father should deny black son. These are grave crimes indeed, and we have committed them and continue to commit them in order to make money.

The play then, for me, takes place in Plaguetown, U.S.A., now. The plague is race, the plague is our concept of Christianity: and this raging plague has the power to destroy every human relationship. I once took a short trip with Medgar Evers to the back-woods of Mississippi. He was investigating the murder of a Negro man by a white storekeeper which had taken place months before. Many people talked to Medgar that night, in dark cabins, with their lights out, in whispers; and we had been followed for many miles out of Jackson, Mississippi, not by a lunatic with a gun, but by state troopers. I will never forget that night, as I will never forget Medgar—who took me to the plane the next day. We promised to see each other soon. When he died, something entered into me which I cannot describe, but it was then that I resolved that nothing under heaven would prevent me from getting this play done. We are walking in terrible darkness here, and this is one man's attempt to bear witness to the reality and the power of light.

*James Baldwin*
*New York, April, 1964*

## Cast of Characters
### (in order of appearance)

MERIDIAN HENRY ------------------------------------- *a Negro minister*

TOM

KEN

ARTHUR

JUANITA ⎫ ------------------------------------- *Negro students*

LORENZO

PETE

MOTHER HENRY ------------------------------ *Meridian Henry's mother*

LYLE BRITTEN ------------------------------ *a white store-owner*

JO BRITTEN --------------------------------------- *Lyle's wife*

PARNELL JAMES ------------------------ *editor of the local newspaper*

RICHARD -------------------------------- *Meridian Henry's son*

PAPA D. --------------------------------- *owner of a juke joint*

HAZEL

LILLIAN

SUSAN

RALPH ⎫ ------------------------------- *white townspeople*

ELLIS

REV. PHELPS

GEORGE

THE STATE

COUNSEL FOR THE BEREAVED

Congregation of Rev. Henry's church, Pallbearers, Blacktown, Whitetown

Act I

MULTIPLE SET, the skeleton of which, in the first two acts, is the Negro church, and, in the third act, the courthouse. The church and the courthouse are on opposite sides of a southern street; the audience should always be aware, during the first two acts, of the dome of the courthouse and the American flag. During the final act, the audience should always be aware of the steeple of the church, and the cross.

The church is divided by an aisle. The street door upstage faces the audience. The pulpit is downstage, at an angle, so that the minister is simultaneously addressing the congregation and the audience. In the third act, the pulpit is replaced by the witness stand.

This aisle also functions as the division between WHITETOWN and BLACKTOWN. The action among the blacks takes place on one side of the stage, the action among the whites on the opposite side of the stage—which is to be remembered during the third act, which takes place, of course, in a segregated courtroom.

This means that RICHARD's room, LYLE's store, PAPA D.'s joint, JO's kitchen, etc., are to exist principally by suggestion, for these shouldn't be allowed to obliterate the skeleton, or, more accurately, perhaps, the framework, suggested above.

For the murder scene, the aisle functions as a gulf. The stage should be built out, so that the audience reacts to the enormity of this gulf, and so that RICHARD, when he falls, falls out of sight of the audience, like a stone, into the pit.

In the darkness we hear a shot.

Lights up slowly on LYLE, staring down at the ground. He looks around him, bends slowly and picks up RICHARD's body as though it were a sack. He carries him upstage drops him.

LYLE: And may every nigger like this nigger end like this nigger— face down in the weeds!

(*Exits.* BLACKTOWN: *The church. A sound of mourning begins. Meridian, Tom, Ken and Arthur.*)

MERIDIAN: No, no, no! You have to say it like you mean it—the way they really say it: nigger, nigger, nigger! *Nigger!* Tom, the way *you* saying it, it sounds like you just *might* want to make friends. And that's not the way they sound out there. Remember all that's happened. Remember we having a funeral here—tomorrow night. Remember why. Go on, hit it again.

TOM: You dirty nigger, you no-good black bastard, what you doing down here, anyway?

MERIDIAN: That's much better. Much, much better. Go on.

TOM: Hey, boy, where's your mother? I bet she's lying up in bed, just a-pumping away, ain't she, boy?

MERIDIAN: *That's* the way they sound!

TOM: Hey, boy, how much does your mother charge? How much does your sister charge?

2

KEN: How much does your *wife* charge?

MERIDIAN: Now you got it. You really got it now. That's them. Keep walking, Arthur. *Keep walking!*

TOM: You get your ass off these streets from around here, boy, or we going to do us some cutting—we're going to cut that big, black thing off of you, you hear?

MERIDIAN: Why you all standing around there like that? Go on and get you a nigger. Go on!

(*A scuffle.*)

MERIDIAN: All right. All right! Come on, now. Come on.

(*Ken steps forward and spits in Arthur's face.*)

ARTHUR: You black s.o.b., what the hell do you think you're doing? You mother—!

MERIDIAN: Hey, hold it! Hold it! Hold it!

(*Meridian wipes the boy's face. They are all trembling.*)

(*Mother Henry enters.*)

MOTHER HENRY: Here they come. And it looks like they had a time.

(*Juanita, Lorenzo, Pete, Jimmy, all Negro, carry plac-ards, enter, exhausted and dishevelled, wounded; Pete is weeping. The placards bear such legends as* Freedom Now, We Want The Murderer, One Man, One Vote, *etc.*)

JUANITA: We shall overcome!

LORENZO: We shall not be moved! (*Laughs*) We were moved to-night, though. Some of us has been moved to *tears*.

MERIDIAN: Juanita, what happened?

JUANITA: Oh, just another hometown Saturday night.

MERIDIAN: Come on, Pete, come on, old buddy. Stop it. Stop it.

LORENZO: I don't blame him. I do not blame the cat. You feel like a damn fool standing up there, letting them white mothers beat on your ass—shoot, if I had my way, just once—stop cry-ing, Pete, goddammit!

3

JUANITA: Lorenzo, you're in church.

LORENZO: Yeah. Well, I wish to God I was in an arsenal. I'm sorry, Meridian, Mother Henry—I don't mean that for you. I don't understand you. I don't understand Meridian here. It was his son, it was your grandson, Mother Henry, that got killed, butchered! Just last week, and yet, here you sit—in this—this—the house of this damn almighty God who don't care what happens to nobody, unless, of course, they're white. Mother Henry, I got a lot of respect for you and all that, and for Meridian, too, but that white man's God is *white*. It's that damn white God that's been lynching us and burning us and castrating us and raping our women and robbing us of everything that makes a man a man for all these hundreds of years. Now, why we sitting around here, in *His* house? If I could get my hands on Him, I'd pull Him out of heaven and drag Him through this town at the end of a rope.

MERIDIAN: No, you wouldn't.

LORENZO: I wouldn't? Yes, I would. Oh, yes, I would.

JUANITA: And then you wouldn't be any better than they are.

LORENZO: I don't want to be better than they are, why should I be better than they are? And better at what? Better at being a doormat, better at being a corpse? Sometimes I just don't know. We've been demonstrating—*non-violently*—for more than a year now and all that's happened is that now they'll let us into that crummy library downtown which was obsolete in 1897 and where nobody goes anyway; who in this town reads books? For that we paid I don't know how many thousands of dollars in fines, Jerome is still in the hospital, and we all know that Ruthie is never again going to be the swinging little chick she used to be. Big deal. Now we're picketing that great movie palace downtown where I wouldn't go on a bet; I can live without Yul Brynner and Doris Day,

4

thank you very much. And we *still* can't get licensed to be electricians or plumbers, we still can't walk through the park, our kids still can't use the swimming pool in town. We still can't vote, we can't even get registered. Is it worth it? And these people trying to kill us, too? And we ain't even got no guns. The cops ain't going to protect us. They call up the people and tell them where we are and say, "Go get them! They ain't going to do nothing to you—they just dumb niggers!"

MERIDIAN: Did they arrest anybody tonight?

PETE: No, they got their hands full now, trying to explain what Richard's body was doing in them weeds.

LORENZO: It was wild. You know, all the time we was ducking them bricks and praying to *God* we'd get home before somebody got killed— (*Laughs*) I had a jingle going through my mind, like if I was a white man, dig? and I had to wake up every morning singing to myself, "Look at the happy nigger, he doesn't give a damn, thank God I'm not a nigger—"

TOGETHER: "—*Good Lord, perhaps I am!*"

JUANITA: You've gone crazy, Lorenzo. They've done it. You have been unfitted for the struggle.

MERIDIAN: I cannot rest until they bring my son's murderer to trial. That man who killed my son.

LORENZO: But he killed a nigger before, as I know all of you know. Nothing never happened. Sheriff just shovelled the body into the ground and forgot about it.

MERIDIAN: Parnell will help me.

PETE: Meridian, you know that *Mister* Parnell ain't going to let them arrest his ass-hole buddy. I'm sorry, Mother Henry!

MOTHER HENRY: That's all right, son.

MERIDIAN: But I think that Parnell has proven to be a pretty good friend to all of us. He's the only white man in this town who's ever *really* stuck his neck out in order to do—to do right. He's *fought* to bring about this trial—I can't tell you how hard he's fought. If it weren't for him, there'd be much less hope.

LORENZO: I guess I'm just not as nice as you are. I don't trust as many people as you trust.

MERIDIAN: We can't afford to become too distrustful, Lorenzo.

LORENZO: We can't afford to be too trusting, either. See, when a white man's a *good* white man, he's good because he wants *you* to be good. Well, sometimes I just might want to be *bad*. I got as much right to be bad as anybody else.

MERIDIAN: No, you don't.

LORENZO: Why not?

MERIDIAN: Because you know better.

(*Parnell enters.*)

PARNELL: Hello, my friends. I bring glad tidings of great joy. Is that the way the phrase goes, Meridian?

JUANITA: Parnell!

PARNELL: I can't stay. I just came to tell you that a warrant's being issued for Lyle's arrest.

JUANITA: They're going to arrest him? Big Lyle Britten? I'd love to know how you managed *that*.

PARNELL: Well, Juanita, I am not a *good* man, but I have my little ways.

JUANITA: And a whole lot of folks in this town, baby, are not going to be talking to you no more, for days and days and *days*.

PARNELL: I hope that you all will. I may have no other company. I think I should go to Lyle's house to warn him. After all, I brought it about and he *is* a friend of mine—and then I have to get the announcement into my paper.

JUANITA: So it *is* true.

PARNELL: Oh, yes. It's true.

MERIDIAN: When is he being arrested?

PARNELL: Monday morning. Will you be up later, Meridian? I'll drop by if you are—if I may.

MERIDIAN: Yes. I'll be up.

PARNELL: All right, then. I'll trundle by. Good night all. I'm sorry I've got to run.

MERIDIAN: Good night.

JUANITA: Thank you, Parnell.

PARNELL: Don't thank me, dear Juanita. I only acted—as I believed I had to act. See you later, Meridian.

*(Parnell exits.)*

MERIDIAN: I wonder if they'll convict him.

JUANITA: Convict him. Convict him. You're asking for heaven on earth. After all, they haven't even *arrested* him yet. And, anyway—why *should* they convict him? Why him? He's no worse than all the others. He's an honorable tribesman and he's defended, with blood, the honor and purity of his tribe!

*(WHITETOWN: Lyle holds his infant son up above his head.)*

LYLE: Hey old pisser. You hear me, sir? I expect you to control your bladder like a *gentleman* whenever your Papa's got you on his knee.
*(Jo enters.)*
He got a mighty big bladder, too, for such a little fellow.

JO: I'll tell the world he didn't steal it.

LYLE: You mighty sassy tonight.
*(Hands her the child.)*
Ain't that right, old pisser? Don't you reckon your Mama's getting kind of sassy? And what do you reckon I should do about it?

7

*(Jo is changing the child's diapers.)*

JO: You tell your Daddy he can start sleeping in his own bed nights instead of coming grunting in here in the wee small hours of the morning.

LYLE: And you tell your Mama if she was getting her sleep like she should be, so she can be alert every instant to your needs, little fellow, she wouldn't *know* what time I come—*grunting* in.

JO: I got to be alert to *your* needs, too. I think.

LYLE: Don't you go starting to imagine things. I just been over to the store. That's all.

JO: Till three and four o'clock in the morning?

LYLE: Well, I got plans for the store, I think I'm going to try to start branching out, you know, and I been—making plans.

JO: You thinking of branching out *now?* Why, Lyle, you know we ain't *hardly* doing no business *now*. Weren't for the country folks come to town every Saturday, I don't know *where* we'd be. This ain't no time to be branching *out*. We barely holding *on*.

LYLE: Shoot, the niggers'll be coming back, don't you worry. They'll get over this foolishness presently. They already weary of having to drive forty-fifty miles across the state line to get their groceries—a lot of them ain't even got cars.

JO: Those that don't have cars have *friends* with cars.

LYLE: Well, friends get weary, too. Joel come in the store a couple of days ago—

JO: Papa D.? He don't count. You can always wrap him around your little finger.

LYLE: Listen, will you? He come in the store a couple of days ago to buy a sack of flour and he *told* me, he say, The niggers is *tired* running all over creation to put some food on the table. Ain't nobody going to keep on driving no forty-fifty miles to buy no sack of flour—what you mean when you say Joel don't count?

JO: I don't mean nothing. But there's something wrong with anybody when his own people don't think much of him.

LYLE: Joel's got good sense, is all. I think more of him than I think of a lot of white men, that's a fact. And he knows what's right for his people, too.

JO (*Puts son in crib*): Well. Selling a sack of flour once a week ain't going to send this little one through college, neither. (*A pause*) In what direction were you planning to branch out?

LYLE: I was thinking of trying to make the store more—well, more colorful. Folks like color—

JO: You mean, niggers like color.

LYLE: Dammit, Jo, I ain't in business just to sell to niggers! Listen to me, can't you? I thought I'd dress it up, get a new front, put some neon signs in—and, you know, we got more space in there than we use. Well, why don't we open up a line of ladies' clothes? Nothing too fancy, but I bet you it would bring in a lot more business.

JO: I don't know. Most of the ladies I know buy their clothes at Benton's, on Decatur Street.

LYLE: The niggers don't—anyway, we could sell them the same thing. The white ladies, I mean—

JO: No. It wouldn't be the same.

LYLE: Why not? A dress is a dress.

JO: But it sounds better if you say you got it on Decatur Street! At Benton's. Anyway—where would you get the money for this branching out?

LYLE: I can get a loan from the bank. I'll get old Parnell to co-sign with me, or have him get one of his rich friends to co-sign with me.

JO: Parnell called earlier—you weren't at the store today.

LYLE: What do you mean, I wasn't at the store?

JO: Because Parnell called earlier and said he tried to get you at the store and that there wasn't any answer.

LYLE: There wasn't any business. I took a walk.

JO: He said he's got bad news for you.

LYLE: What kind of bad news?

JO: He didn't say. He's coming by here this evening to give it to you himself.

LYLE: What do you think it is?

JO: I guess they're going to arrest you?

LYLE: No, they ain't. They ain't gone crazy.

JO: I think they might. We had so much trouble in this town lately and it's been in all the northern newspapers—and now, this —this dead boy—

LYLE: They ain't got no case.

JO: No. But you was the last person to see that crazy boy—alive. And now everybody's got to thinking again—about that other time.

LYLE: That was self defense. The Sheriff said so himself. Hell, I ain't no murderer. They're just some things I don't believe is right.

JO: Nobody never heard no more about the poor little girl—his wife.

LYLE: No. She just disappeared.

JO: You never heard no more about her at all?

LYLE: How would I hear about her more than anybody else? No, she just took off—I believe she had people in Detroit some-where. I reckon that's where she went.

JO: I felt sorry for her. She looked so lost those last few times I saw her, wandering around town—and she was so young. She was a pretty little thing.

LYLE: She looked like a pickaninny to me. Like she was too young to be married. I reckon she *was* too young for him.

JO: It happened in the store.

LYLE: Yes.

JO: How people talked! That's what scares me now.

LYLE: Talk don't matter. I hope you didn't believe what you heard.

JO: A lot of people did. I reckon a lot of people still do.

LYLE: *You* don't believe it?

JO: No. (*A pause*) You know—Monday morning—we'll be married one whole year!

LYLE: Well, can't nobody talk about *us*. That little one there ain't but two months old.

(*The door bell rings.*)

JO: That's Parnell.

(*Exits.*)

(*Lyle walks up and down, looks into the crib. Jo and Parnell enter.*)

LYLE: It's about time you showed your face in here, you old rascal! You been so busy over there with the niggers, you ain't got time for white folks no more. You sure you ain't got some nigger wench over there on the other side of town? Because, I declare—!

PARNELL: I apologize for your husband, Mrs. Britten, I really do. In fact, I'm afraid I must deplore your taste in men. If I had only seen you first, dear lady, and if you had found me charming, how much suffering I might have prevented! You got anything in this house to drink? Don't tell me you haven't, we'll both need one. Sit down.

LYLE: Bring on the booze, old lady.

(*Jo brings ice, glasses, etc.; pours drinks.*)

What you been doing with yourself?

PARNELL: Well, I seem to have switched territories. I haven't been defending colored people this week, I've been defending you. I've just left the Chief of Police.

LYLE: How is the old bastard?

PARNELL: He seems fine. But he really *is* an old bastard. Lyle—he's issuing a warrant for your arrest.

LYLE: He's going to arrest *me*? You mean, he believes I killed that boy?

PARNELL: The question of what he believes doesn't enter into it. This case presents several very particular circumstances and these circumstances force him to arrest you. I think we can take it for granted that he wouldn't arrest you if he could think of some way not to. He wouldn't arrest anybody except blind beggars and old colored women if he could think of some way not to—he's bird-brained and chicken-hearted and big-assed. The charge is murder.

JO: Murder!

LYLE: Murder?

PARNELL: Murder.

LYLE: I ain't no murderer. You know that.

PARNELL: I also know that somebody killed the boy. Somebody put two slugs in his belly and dumped his body in the weeds beside the railroad track just outside of town. Somebody did all that. We pay several eminent, bird-brained, chicken-hearted, big-assed people quite a lot of money to discourage such activity. They never do, in fact, discourage it, but, still —we must find the somebody who killed that boy. And you, my friend, according to the testimony of Joel Davis, otherwise known as Papa D., were the last person to see the boy alive. It is also known that you didn't like him—to say the least.

LYLE: Nobody liked him.

PARNELL: Ah. But it isn't nobody that killed him. *Somebody* killed him. We must find the somebody. And since you were the last person to see him alive, we must arrest you in order to clear you—or convict you.

LYLE: They'll never convict me.

PARNELL: As to that, you may be right. But you *are* going to be arrested.

LYLE: When?

PARNELL: Monday morning. Of course, you can always flee to Mexico.

LYLE: Why should I run away?

PARNELL: I wasn't suggesting that you should run away. If you did, I should urge your wife to divorce you at once, and marry me.

JO: Ah, if that don't get him out of town in a hurry, I don't know what will! The man's giving you your chance, honey. You going to take it?

LYLE: Stop talking foolishness. It looks bad for me, I guess. I swear, I don't know what's come over the folks in this town!

PARNELL: It doesn't look good. In fact, if the boy had been white, it would look very, *very* bad, and your behind would be in the jail house now. What do you mean, you don't understand what's come over the people in this town?

LYLE: Raising so much fuss about a nigger—and a northern nigger at that.

PARNELL: He was born here. He's Reverend Meridian Henry's son.

LYLE: Well, he'd been gone so long, he might as well have been a northern nigger. Went North and got ruined and come back here to make trouble—and they tell me he was a dope fiend, too. What's all this fuss about? He probably got killed by some other nigger—they do it all the time—but ain't nobody

13

even thought about arresting one of *them*. Has niggers suddenly got to be *holy* in this town?

PARNELL: Oh, Lyle, I'm not here to discuss the sanctity of niggers. I just came to tell you that a warrant's being issued for your arrest. *You* may think that a colored boy who gets ruined in the North and then comes home to try to pull himself together deserves to die—*I* don't.

LYLE: You sound like you think I got something against colored folks—but I don't. I never have, not in all my life. But I'll be damned if I'll mix with them. That's all. I don't believe in it, and that's *all*. I don't want no big buck nigger lying up next to Josephine and that's where all this will lead to and you know it as well as I do! I'm against it and I'll do anything I have to do to stop it, yes, I will!

PARNELL: Suppose *he*—my godson there—decides to marry a Chinese girl. You know, there are an awful lot of Chinese girls in the world—I bet you didn't know that. Well, there are. Let's just say that he grows up and looks around at all the pure white women, and—saving your presence, ma'am—they make him want to puke and he decides to marry a pure Chinese girl instead. What would you do? Shoot him in order to prevent it? Or would you shoot her?

LYLE: Parnell, you're my buddy. You've *always* been my buddy. You know more about me than anybody else in the world. What's come over you? You—you ain't going to turn against me, are you?

PARNELL: No. No, I'll never turn against you. I'm just trying to make you think.

LYLE: I notice you didn't marry no Chinese girl. You just never got married at all. Women been trying to saddle old Parnell for I don't know how long—I don't know what you got, old buddy, but I'll be damned if you don't know how to use it!

What about this present one—Loretta—you reckon you goi
to marry her?

PARNELL: I doubt it.

JO: Parnell, you're just awful. Awful!

PARNELL: I think I'm doing her a favor. She can do much be
than me. I'm just a broken-down newspaper editor—the
tor of a newspaper which *nobody* reads—in a dim, 
backwater.

LYLE: I thought you liked it here.

PARNELL: I don't like it here. But I love it here. Or maybe I d
I don't know. I must go.

LYLE: What's your hurry? Why don't you stay and have pot
with us?

PARNELL: Loretta is waiting. I must have pot-luck with *her*.
then I have errands on the other side of town.

LYLE: What they saying over there? I reckon they praying da
night for my ass to be put in a sling, ain't they? Sh
don't care.

PARNELL: Don't. Life's much simpler that way. Anyway, Pap
the only one doing a whole lot of talking.

JO: I told you he wasn't no good, Lyle, I told you!

LYLE: I don't know what's got into him! And we been kı
each other all these years! He must be getting old. 
back and tell him I said he's got it all *confused*—ab
and that boy. Tell him you talked to me and that *I*
must have made some mistake.

PARNELL: I'll drop in tomorrow, if I may. Good night, Jo, an
you. Good night, Lyle.

LYLE: Good night, old buddy.

JO: I'll see you to the door.

(*Jo and Parnell exit. Lyle walks up and down.*)

15

LYLE: Well! *Ain't* that something! But they'll never convict me. Never in this world. (*Looks into crib*) Ain't that right, old pisser?

(BLACKTOWN: *The church, as before.*)

LORENZO: And when they bring him to trial, I'm going to be there every day—right across the street in that courthouse—where they been dealing death out to us for all these years.

MOTHER HENRY: I used to hate them, too, son. But I don't hate them no more. They too pitiful.

MERIDIAN: No witnesses.

JUANITA: Meridian. Ah, Meridian.

MOTHER HENRY: You remember that song he used to like so much?

MERIDIAN: I sing because I'm happy.

JUANITA: I sing because I'm free.

PETE: For his eye is on the sparrow—

LORENZO: And I know he watches—me.

(*Music, very faint*)

JUANITA: There was another song he liked—a song about a prison and the light from a train that shone on the prisoners every night at midnight. I can hear him now: Lord, you wake up in the morning. You hear the ding-dong ring—

MOTHER HENRY: He had a beautiful voice.

LORENZO: Well, he was pretty tough up there in New York—till he got busted.

MERIDIAN: And came running home.

MOTHER HENRY: Don't blame yourself, honey. Don't blame yourself!

JUANITA: You go a-marching to the table, you see the same old thing—

JIMMY: All I'm going to tell you: knife, a fork, and a pan—

(*Music stronger*)

16

PETE: And if you say a thing about it—

LORENZO: You are in trouble with the man.

> (*Lights dim in the church. We discover Richard, standing in his room, singing. This number is meant to make vivid the Richard who was much loved on the Apollo Theatre stage in Harlem, the Richard who was a rising New York star.*)

MERIDIAN: No witnesses!

> (*Near the end of the song, Mother Henry enters, carrying a tray with milk, sandwiches, and cake.*)

RICHARD: You treating me like royalty, old lady—I ain't royalty. I'm just a raggedy-assed, out-of-work, busted musician. But I sure can sing, can't I?

MOTHER HENRY: You better learn some respect, you know that neither me nor your father wants that kind of language in this house. Sit down and eat, you got to get your strength back.

RICHARD: What for? What am I supposed to do with it?

MOTHER HENRY: You stop that kind of talk.

RICHARD: Stop that kind of talk, we don't want that kind of talk! Nobody cares what people feel or what they think or what they do—but stop that kind of talk!

MOTHER HENRY: Richard!

RICHARD: All right. All right. (*Throws himself on the bed, begins eating in a kind of fury.*) What I can't get over is—what in the world am I doing *here*? Way down here in the ass-hole of the world, the deep, black, funky South.

MOTHER HENRY: You were born here. You got folks here. And you ain't got no manners and you *won't* learn no sense and so you naturally got yourself in trouble and had to come to your folks. You lucky it wasn't no worse, the way you go on. You want some more milk?

RICHARD: No, old lady. Sit down.

MOTHER HENRY: I ain't got time to be fooling with you. (*But she sits down.*) What you got on your mind?

RICHARD: I don't know. How do you stand it?

MOTHER HENRY: Stand what? You?

RICHARD: Living down here with all these nowhere people.

MOTHER HENRY: From what I'm told and from what I see, the people you've been among don't seem to be any better.

RICHARD: You mean old Aunt Edna? She's all right, she just ain't very bright, is all.

MOTHER HENRY: I am not talking about Edna. I'm talking about all them other folks you got messed up with. Look like you'd have had better sense. You hear me?

RICHARD: I hear you.

MOTHER HENRY: That all you got to say?

RICHARD: It's easy for you to talk, Grandmama, you don't know nothing about New York City, or what can happen to you up there!

MOTHER HENRY: I know what can happen to you anywhere in this world. And I know right from wrong. We tried to raise you so you'd know right from wrong, too.

RICHARD: We don't see things the same way, Grandmama. I don't know if I really *know* right from wrong—I'd like to, I always dig people the most who know *anything*, especially right from wrong!

MOTHER HENRY: You've had yourself a little trouble, Richard, like we all do, and you a little tired, like we all get. You'll be all right. You a young man. Only, just try not to *go* so much, try to calm down a little. Your Daddy loves you. You his only son.

18

RICHARD: That's a good reason, Grandmama. Let me tell you about New York. You ain't never been North, have you?

MOTHER HENRY: Your Daddy used to tell me a little about it every time he come back from visiting you all up there.

RICHARD: Daddy don't know nothing about New York. He just come up for a few days and went right on back. That ain't the way to get to know New York. No ma'am. He *never* saw New York. Finally, I realized he wasn't never *going* to see it—you know, there's a whole lot of things Daddy's never seen? I've seen more than he has.

MOTHER HENRY: All young folks thinks that.

RICHARD: Did *you*? When you were young? Did you think you knew more than your mother and father? But I bet you really did, you a pretty shrewd old lady, quiet as it's kept.

MOTHER HENRY: No, I didn't think that. But I thought I could find *out* more, because *they* were born in slavery, but *I* was born free.

RICHARD: *Did* you find out more?

MOTHER HENRY: I found out what I had to find out—to take care of my husband and raise my children in the fear of God.

RICHARD: You know I don't believe in God, Grandmama.

MOTHER HENRY: You don't know what you talking about. Ain't no way possible for you not to believe in God. It ain't up to you.

RICHARD: Who's it up to, then?

MOTHER HENRY: It's up to the life in you—the life in you. *That* knows where it comes from, *that* believes in God. You doubt me, you just try holding your breath long enough to die.

RICHARD: You pretty smart, ain't you? (*A pause*) I convinced Daddy that I'd be better off in New York—and Edna, she convinced him too, she said it wasn't as tight for a black man up there as it is down here. Well, that's a crock, Grandmama, believe me when I tell you. At first I thought it was true, hell, I was just a green country boy and they ain't got no signs up, dig, saying you can't go here or you can't go there. No, you got to find that out all by your lonesome. But—for awhile—I thought everything was swinging and Edna, she's so dizzy she thinks everything is *always* swinging, so there we were—like *swinging*.

MOTHER HENRY: I know Edna got lost somewhere. But, Richard—why didn't *you* come back? You knew your Daddy wanted you back, your Daddy and me both.

RICHARD: I didn't want to come back here like a whipped dog. One whipped dog running to another whipped dog. No, I didn't want that. I wanted to make my Daddy proud of me—because, the day I left here, I sure as hell wasn't proud of *him*.

MOTHER HENRY: Be careful, son. Be careful. Your Daddy's a fine man. Your Daddy loves you.

RICHARD: I know, Grandmama. But I just wish, that day that Mama died, he'd took a pistol and gone through that damn white man's hotel and shot every son of a bitch in the place. That's right. I wish he'd shot them dead. I been dreaming of that day ever since I left here. I been dreaming of my Mama falling down the steps of that hotel. *My* Mama. I never believed she fell. I *always* believed that some white man pushed her down those steps. And I know that Daddy thought so, too. But he wasn't there, he didn't know, he couldn't say nothing, he couldn't *do* nothing. I'll never forget the way he looked—whipped, whipped, whipped, whipped!

MOTHER HENRY: She fell, Richard, she *fell*. The stairs were wet and slippery and she *fell*.

RICHARD: My mother *fell* down the steps of that damn white hotel? My mother was *pushed*—you remember yourself how them white bastards was always sniffing around my mother, *always* around her—because she was pretty and *black!*

MOTHER HENRY: Richard, you can't start walking around believing that all the suffering in the world is caused by white folks!

RICHARD: I can't? Don't tell me I can't. I'm going to treat everyone of them as though they were responsible for all the crimes that ever happened in the history of the world—oh, yes! They're responsible for all the misery *I've* ever seen, and that's good enough for me. It's because my Daddy's got no power that my Mama's dead. And he ain't got no power because he's *black.* And the only way the black man's going to *get* any power is to drive all the white men into the sea.

MOTHER HENRY: You're going to make yourself sick. You're going to make yourself sick with hatred.

RICHARD: No, I'm not. I'm going to make myself well. I'm going to make myself *well* with hatred—what do you think of that?

MOTHER HENRY: It can't be done. It can never be done. Hatred is a poison, Richard.

RICHARD: Not for me. I'm going to learn how to drink it—a little every day in the morning, and then a booster shot late at night. I'm going to remember everything. I'm going to keep it right here, at the very top of my mind. I'm going to remember Mama, and Daddy's face that day, and Aunt Edna and all her sad little deals and all those boys and girls in Harlem and all them pimps and whores and gangsters and all them cops. And I'm going to remember all the dope that's flowed through my veins. I'm going to remember everything —the jails I been in and the cops that beat me and how long a time I spent screaming and stinking in my own dirt, trying to break my habit. I'm going to remember all that, and I'll get well. I'll get well.

MOTHER HENRY: Oh, Richard. Richard. Richard.

RICHARD: Don't Richard *me.* I tell you, I'm going to get *well.*

(*He takes a small, sawed-off pistol from his pocket.*)

MOTHER HENRY: Richard, what are you doing with that gun?

RICHARD: I'm carrying it around with me, that's what I'm doing with it. This gun goes everywhere I go.

MOTHER HENRY: How long have you had it?

RICHARD: I've had it a long, long time.

MOTHER HENRY: Richard—you never—?

RICHARD: No. Not yet. But I will when I have to. I'll sure as hell take one of the bastards with me.

MOTHER HENRY: Hand me that gun. Please.

RICHARD: I can't. This is all that the man understands. He don't understand nothing else. *Nothing else!*

MOTHER HENRY: Richard—your father—think of your father—

RICHARD: Don't tell him! You hear me? (*A pause*) Don't tell him!

MOTHER HENRY: Richard. Please.

RICHARD: Take the tray away, old lady. I ain't hungry no more.

(*After a moment, Mother Henry takes the tray and exits. Richard stretches out on the bed.*)

JUANITA (*Off*): Meridian? Mother Henry? Anybody home in this house? (*Enters*) Oh! Excuse me.

RICHARD: I think they might be over at the church. I reckon Grandmama went over there to pray for my soul.

JUANITA: Grandmama?

RICHARD: Who are you? Don't I know you?

JUANITA: Yes. I think you might.

RICHARD: Is your name Juanita?

JUANITA: If your name is Richard.

RICHARD: I'll be damned.

JUANITA: Ain't you a mess? So you finally decided to come back here—come here, let me hug you! Why, you ain't hardly changed at all—you just a little taller but you sure didn't gain much weight.

RICHARD: And I bet you the same old tomboy. You sure got the same loud voice—used to be able to hear you clear across this town.

JUANITA: Well, it's a mighty small town, Richard, that's what you always said—and the reason my voice got so loud so early, was that I started screaming for help right quick.

*(Pete enters.)*

Do you know Pete Spivey? He's someone come on the scene since you been gone. He's going to school down here, you should pardon the expression.

RICHARD: How do you do, man? Where you from?

PETE: I'm from a little place just outside Mobile.

RICHARD: Why didn't you go North, man? If you was going to make a *move. That's* the place. You get lost up there and I guarantee you some swinging little chick is sure to find you.

JUANITA: We'll let that pass. Are you together? Are you ready to meet the day?

RICHARD: I am *always* together, little sister. Tell me what you got on your mind.

PETE: We thought we'd just walk around town a little and maybe stop and have a couple of drinks somewhere. Or we can drive. I got a car.

RICHARD: I didn't think I'd never see you no more, Juanita. You been here all this time?

JUANITA: I sure have, sugar. Just waiting for you to come home.

RICHARD: Don't let this chick upset you, Pete. All we ever did was climb trees together.

23

PETE: She's had me climbing a few trees, too. But we weren't doing it together.

(PAPA D.'S JUKE JOINT: *Juke box music, loud. Less frantic than Richard's song. Couples dancing, all very young, doing very lively variations of the "Twist," the "Wobble," etc. Papa D. at the counter. It is now early evening. Juanita, Pete and Richard enter.*)

JUANITA: How you making it, Papa D.? We brought someone to see you—you recognize him?

PAPA D.: It seems to me I know your face, young man. Yes, I'm *sure* I know your face. Now, wait a minute, don't tell me—you ain't Shirelee Anderson's boy, are you?

RICHARD: No. I remember Shirelee Anderson, but we ain't no kin.

PETE: Try again, Papa D.

PAPA D.: You your father's boy. I just recognized that smile—you Reverend Henry's son. Well, how you doing? It's nice to have you back with us. You going to stay awhile?

RICHARD: Yes sir. I think I'll be around for awhile.

PAPA D.: Yeah, I remember you little old string bean of a boy, full of the devil. How long you been gone from here?

RICHARD: Almost eight years now. I left in September—it'll be eight years next month.

PAPA D.: Yeah—how's your Daddy? And your Grandmother? I ain't seen them for awhile.

PETE: Ain't you been going to church, Papa D.?

PAPA D.: Well, you know how it is. I try, God *knows* I try!

RICHARD: They fine, Papa D.

PAPA D.: You all don't want nothing to eat?

RICHARD: We'll think about it.

(*They sit down.*)

PETE: Old Papa D. got something on everybody, don't he?

JUANITA: You better believe it.

RICHARD: He's kind of a Tom, ain't he?

PETE: Yeah. He *talks* about Mister Charlie, and he *says* he's with us—us kids—but he ain't going to do nothing to offend him. You know, he's still trading with Lyle Britten.

RICHARD: Who's Lyle Britten?

PETE: Peckerwood, owns a store nearby. And, man, you ain't *seen* a peckerwood until you've seen Lyle Britten. Niggers been trading in his store for years, man, I wouldn't be surprised but if the cat was rich—but that man still expects you to step off the sidewalk when he comes along. So we been getting people to stop buying there.

JUANITA: He shot a colored man a few years back, shot him dead, and wasn't nothing never said, much less done, about it.

PETE: Lyle had been carrying on with this man's wife, dig, and, naturally, Old Bill—his name was Bill Walker, everybody called him Old Bill—wanted to put a stop to it.

JUANITA: She was a pretty little thing—real little and real black.

RICHARD: She still around here?

PETE: No. She disappeared. She went North somewhere.

RICHARD: Jive mothers. They can rape and kill our women and we can't do nothing. But if we touch one of their dried-up, pale-assed women, we get our nuts cut off. You remember that chick I was telling you about earlier, lives in Greenwich Village in New York?

PETE: What about her?

RICHARD: She's *white,* man. I got a whole *gang* of white chicks in New York. That's *right.* And they can't get enough of what little Richard's got—and I give it to them, too, baby, believe me. You say black people ain't got no dignity? Man, you

25

ought to watch a white woman when she wants you to give her a little bit. They will do anything, baby *anything!* Wait —I got some pictures. That's the one lives in the Village. *Ain't* she fine? I'd hate to tell you where I've had that long yellow hair. And, dig this one, this is Sandy, her old man works on Wall Street—

PETE: We're making Juanita nervous.

JUANITA: Don't worry about *me*. I've been a big girl for a *long* time. Besides, I'm studying abnormal psychology. So please feel free. Which one is this? What does *her* father do?

RICHARD: That's Sylvia. I don't know what her father does. She's a model. She's loaded with loot.

PETE: You take money from her?

RICHARD: I take their money and they love it. Anyway, they ain't got nothing else to do with it. Every one of them's got some piss-assed, faggoty white boy on a string somewhere. They go home and marry him, dig, when they can't make it with me no more—but when they want some *loving*, funky, down-home, bring-it-on-here-and-put-it-on-the-table style—

JUANITA: They sound very sad. It must be very sad for you, too.

RICHARD: Well, I want *them* to be sad, baby, I want to screw up *their* minds *forever*. But why should *I* be so sad? Hell, I was swinging, I just about had it made. I had me some fine chicks and a fine pad and my car, and, hell, I was on my way! But then—then I screwed up.

JUANITA: We heard you were sick.

RICHARD: Who told you I was sick?

JUANITA: Your father. Your grandmother. They didn't say what the sickness was.

*(Papa D. passes their table.)*

RICHARD: Hey, Papa D., come on over here. I want to show you something.

26

*(Papa D. comes over.)*

Hey, look at these, man, look! Ain't they some fine chicks? And you know who *each one* of them calls: *Baby! Oh, baby?* That's right. You looking at the man.

PAPA D.: Where'd you steal those pictures, boy?

RICHARD *(Laughs):* Steal them! Man, I ain't got to steal girls' pictures. I'm telling you the truth!

PAPA D.: Put them pictures away. I thought you had good sense.

*(He goes back to the counter.)*

RICHARD: Ain't that a bitch. He's scared because I'm carrying around pictures of white girls. That's the trouble with niggers. They all scared of the man.

JUANITA: Well, I'm *not* scared of the man. But there's just no point in running around, asking—

PETE: —to be lynched.

RICHARD: Well, okay, I'll put my pictures away, then. I sure don't want to upset nobody.

PETE: Excuse me. I'll be back.

*(Exits.)*

RICHARD: You want to dance?

JUANITA: No. Not now.

RICHARD: You want something to eat?

JUANITA: No. Richard?

RICHARD: Yeah?

JUANITA: Were you *very* sick?

RICHARD: What d'you want to know for?

JUANITA: Like that. Because I used to be your girl friend.

RICHARD: You was more like a boy than a girl, though. I couldn't go nowhere without you. You were determined to get your neck broken.

JUANITA: Well, I've changed. I'm now much more like a girl than I am like a boy.

RICHARD: You didn't turn out too bad, considering what you had to start with.

JUANITA: Thank you. I guess.

RICHARD: How come you ain't married by now? Pete, now, he seems real fond of you.

JUANITA: He *is* fond of me, we're friends. But I'm not in any hurry to get married—not now. And not here. I'm not sure I'm going to stay here. I've been working very hard, but next year I think I'll leave.

RICHARD: Where would you go?

JUANITA: I don't know. I had always intended to go North to law school and then come back down here to practice law—God knows this town could stand it. But, now, I don't know.

RICHARD: It's rough, huh?

JUANITA: It's not that so much. It *is* rough—are you all right? Do you want to go?

RICHARD: No, no. I'm all right. Go on. (*A pause*) I'm all *right*. Go *on.*

JUANITA: It's rough because you can't help being scared. I don't want to die—what was the matter with you, Richard, what were you sick with?

RICHARD: It wasn't serious. And I'm better now.

JUANITA: Well, no, that's just it. You're not really better.

RICHARD: How do you mean?

JUANITA: I watch you—

RICHARD: *Why* do you watch me?

JUANITA: I care about you.

RICHARD: You care about me! I thought you could hold your liquor better than that, girl.

28

JUANITA: It's not liquor. Don't you believe that anyone can care about you?

RICHARD: Care about me! Do you know how many times chicks have told me that? That they *cared* about me?

JUANITA: Well. This isn't one of those times.

RICHARD: I was a junkie.

JUANITA: A what?

RICHARD: A junkie, a dope addict, a hop-head, a mainliner—a dope fiend! My arms and my legs, too, are full of holes!

JUANITA: I asked you tell *me*, not the world.

RICHARD: Where'd Pete go?

JUANITA: He's dancing.

RICHARD: You want to dance?

JUANITA: In a minute.

RICHARD: I got hooked about five years ago. See, I couldn't stand these chicks I was making it with, and I was working real hard at my music, and, man, I was lonely. You come off a gig, you be tired, and you'd already taken as much shit as you could stand from the managers and the people in the room you were working and you'd be off to make some down scene with some pasty white-faced bitch. And so you'd make the scene and somehow you'd wake up in the morning and the chick would be beside you, alive and well, and dying to make the scene again and somehow you'd managed not to strangle her, you hadn't beaten her to death. Like you wanted to. And you get out of there and you carry this pain around inside all day and all night long. No way to beat it— no *way*. No matter how you turned, no matter what you did—no *way*. But when I started getting high, I was cool, and it didn't bother me. And I wasn't lonely then, it was all right. And the chicks—I could handle them, they couldn't reach me. And I didn't know I was hooked—until I was *hooked*. Then I started getting into trouble and I lost a lot of gigs and I had to sell my car and I lost my pad and most of the chicks, they split, naturally—but not all of them—and then I got busted and I made that trip down to Lexington and—here I am. Way *down* upon the Swanee River. But I'm going to be all right. You can bet on it.

JUANITA: I'd like to do better than that. I'd like to see to it.

RICHARD: How?

JUANITA: Well, like I used to. I won't let you go anywhere without me.

RICHARD: You *still* determined to break your neck.

JUANITA: Well, it's a neck-breaking time. I wouldn't like to appear to be above the battle.

RICHARD: Do you have any idea of what you might be letting yourself in for?

JUANITA: No. But you said you were lonely. And I'm lonely, too.

(*Lyle enters, goes to the counter. His appearance causes a change in the atmosphere, but no one appears to stop whatever they are doing.*)

LYLE: Joel, how about letting me have some change for cigarettes? I got a kind of long drive ahead of me, and I'm out.

PAPA D.: Howdy, Mister Lyle, how you been? Folks ain't been seeing much of you lately.

LYLE (*Laughs*): That's the truth. But I reckon old friends just stays old friends. Ain't that right?

PAPA D.: That's right, Mister Lyle.

JUANITA: That's Lyle Britten. The one we were talking about before.

RICHARD: I wonder what he'd do if I walked into a white place.

JUANITA: Don't worry about it. Just stay out of white places—believe me!

RICHARD *(Laughs)*: Let's TCB—that means taking care of business. Let's see if I can dance.

*(They rise, dance. Perhaps she is teaching him the "Fight," or he is teaching her the "Pony"; they are enjoying each other. Lyle gets his change, gets cigarettes out of the machine, crosses to the counter, pauses there to watch the dancers.)*

LYLE: Joel, you know I ain't never going to be able to dance like that.

PAPA D.: Ain't nothing to it. You just got to be supple, that's all. I can *yet* do it.

*(Does a grotesque sketch of the "Twist.")*

LYLE: Okay, Joel, you got it. Be seeing you now.

PAPA D.: Good night, Mister Lyle.

*(On Lyle's way out, he jostles Juanita. Richard stops, holding Juanita at the waist. Richard and Lyle stare at each other.)*

LYLE: Pardon me.

RICHARD: Consider yourself pardoned.

LYLE: You new around here?

PAPA D.: He just come to town a couple of days ago, Mister Lyle.

RICHARD: Yeah. I just come to town a couple of days ago, Mister Lyle.

LYLE: Well. I sure hope your stay'll be a pleasant one.

*(Exits.)*

PETE: Man, are you *anxious* to leave this world? Because he wouldn't think nothing of helping you out of it.

RICHARD: Yeah. Well, I wouldn't think nothing of helping him out of it, neither. Come on, baby, record's going to waste—let's TCB.

*(They dance.)*

31

So you care about me, do you? Ain't that a bitch?

(THE CHURCH: *Pete and Juanita, a little apart from the others.*)

PETE: Why have you been avoiding me? Don't answer that. You started going away from me as soon as Richard came to this town. Now listen, Richard's dead but you still won't turn to me. I don't want to ask you for more than you can give, but why have you locked me out? I *know*—you liked me. We had nice times together.

JUANITA: We did. I *do* like you. Pete, I don't know. I wish you wouldn't ask me now. I wish *nobody* would ask me for anything now!

PETE: Is it because of Richard? Because if that's what it is, I'll wait—I'll wait until you know inside you that Richard's dead, but you're alive, and you're *supposed* to live, and I love you.

JUANITA: When Richard came, he—*hit*—me in someplace where I'd never been touched before. I don't mean—just physically. He took all my attention—the deepest attention, maybe, that one person can give another. He needed me and he made a difference for me in this terrible world—do you see what I mean? And—it's funny—when I was with him, I didn't think of the future, I didn't dare. I didn't know if I could be strong enough to give him what he needed for as long as he would need it. It only lasted four or five days, Pete—four or five days, like a storm, like lightning! And what I saw during that storm I'll always see. Before that—I thought I knew who I was. But now I know that there are more things in me than I'll ever understand—and if I can't be faithful to myself, I'm afraid to promise I'll be faithful to one man!

PETE: I need you. I'll be faithful. That helps. You'll see.

JUANITA: So many people need so much!

PETE: So do you. So do I, Juanita. You take all my attention. My deepest attention.

JUANITA: You probably see things that I think are hidden. You probably think I'm a fool—or worse.

PETE: No. I think there's a lot of love in you, Juanita. If you'll let me help you, we can give it to the world. You can't give it to the world until you find a person who can help you— love the world.

JUANITA: I've discovered that. The world is a loveless place.

PETE: Not yet—

(*The lights of a car flash in their faces. Silence. They all listen tensely as the lights of another car approach, then pass; they watch the lights disappear. The telephone rings in the office. Mother Henry goes off to answer it. They listen to the murmur of Mother Henry's voice. Mother Henry enters.*)

MOTHER HENRY: That was Freddy Roberts. He say about two-thirty his dog started to barking and woke him up and he let the dog out on the porch and the dog run under the porch and there was two white men *under* Freddy's porch, fooling around with his gas pipes. Freddy thinks the dog bit one of them. He ran inside to get him his rifle but the rifle jammed and the men got away. He wanted to warn us, maybe they might come prowling around here.

LORENZO: Only we ain't got no rifles.

JUANITA: It was the dog that woke him up? I'll bet they come back and kill that dog!

JIMMY: What was they doing under the man's house, messing around with his gas pipes, at that hour of the morning?

PETE: They was fixing to blow up his house. They *might* be under your house, or *this* house, right now.

LORENZO: The real question is why two white men feel safe enough to come to a black neighborhood after dark in the first place. If a couple of them get their heads blown off, they won't feel so goddamn courageous!

JUANITA: I better call home.

>   (*Exits into office.*)

PETE: Will you have your mother call my house?

LORENZO: And have *his* mother call *my* house?

JIMMY: And tell all the people that don't have rifles or dogs to stay off their porches!

LORENZO: Tell them to fall on their knees and use their Bibles as breast-plates! Because I know that each and every one of them got *Bibles!* (*Meridian has walked to the church door, stands looking off*)

LORENZO: Don't they, Meridian?

MOTHER HENRY: Hush.

>   (*We hear Juanita's voice, off. Then silence falls. Lights dim on the students until they are in silhouette. Lights up on Meridian. We hear Richard's guitar, very lonely, far away.*)

>   (*A car door slams. The voices of young people saying good night. Richard appears, dressed as we last saw him.*)

RICHARD: Hello, Daddy. You still up?

MERIDIAN: Yeah. Couldn't sleep. How was your day?

RICHARD: It was all right. I'd forgotten what nights down here were like. You never see the stars in the city—and all these funny country sounds—

MERIDIAN: Crickets. And all kinds of bugs and worms, running around, busy, shaking all the bushes.

RICHARD: Lord, if I'd stayed here, I guess I might have married old Juanita by now, and we'd have a couple of kids and I'd be sitting around like this *every* night. What a wild thought.

MERIDIAN: You can still marry Juanita. Maybe she's been waiting for you.

RICHARD: Have you ever thought of marrying again?

MERIDIAN: I've thought of it.

RICHARD: Did you ever think of marrying Juanita?

MERIDIAN: Why do you ask me that?

RICHARD: Because I'd like to know.

MERIDIAN: *Why* would you like to know?

RICHARD: Why would you like to hide it? I'd like to know because I'm a man now, Daddy, and I can ask you to tell me the truth. I'm making up for lost time. Maybe you should try to make up for lost time too.

MERIDIAN: Yes. I've thought of marrying Juanita. But I've never spoken of it to her.

RICHARD: That's the truth?

MERIDIAN: Yes.

RICHARD: Why didn't you tell me the truth way back there? Why didn't you tell me my mother was murdered? She was pushed down them steps.

MERIDIAN: Richard, your mother's dead. People die in all kinds of ways. They die when their times comes to die. Your mother loved you and she was gone—there was nothing more I could do for her. I had to think of you. I didn't want you to be—poisoned—by useless and terrible suspicions. I didn't want to wreck your life. I knew your life was going to be hard enough. So, I let you go. I thought it might be easier for you—if I let you go. I didn't want you to grow up in this town.

RICHARD: But there was something else in it, too, Daddy. You didn't want me to look at you and be ashamed of you. And you didn't know what was in my eyes, you couldn't stand it, I could tell from the way you looked at me sometimes. That was it, wasn't it?

MERIDIAN: I thought it was better. I suppose I thought it was all over for me, anyway. And I thought I owed it to your mother

35

and to girls like your mother, to try—try to change, to purify this town, where she was born, and where we'd been so happy, and which she loved so much. I was wrong, I guess. I was wrong.

RICHARD: You've just been a public man, Daddy, haven't you? Since that day? You haven't been a private man at all.

MERIDIAN: No. I haven't. Try to forgive me.

RICHARD: There's nothing to forgive. I've been down the road a little bit. I know what happened. I'm going to try again, Daddy.

*(A pause. Richard take out the gun.)*

Here. Grandmama saw this this morning and she got all upset. So I'll let you hold it for me. You keep it till I ask you for it, okay? But when I ask you for it, you got to give it to me. Okay?

MERIDIAN *(Takes the gun)*: Okay. I'm proud of how you've come through—all you've had to bear.

RICHARD: I'm going to get some sleep. You coming over to the house now?

MERIDIAN: Not yet.

RICHARD: Good night. Say, Daddy?

MERIDIAN: Yeah?

RICHARD: You kind of like the idea of me and Juanita getting to-gether?

MERIDIAN: Yeah. I think it's a fine idea.

RICHARD: Well, I'm going to sleep on it, then. Good night.

MERIDIAN: Good night.

*(Richard exits.)*

*(After Richard's exit, the lights come up on the students.)*

JUANITA: Lord it's gone and started raining.

PETE: And you worried about your hair.

JUANITA: I am *not* worried about my hair. I'm thinking of wearing it the way God arranged it in the first place.

LORENZO: Now, now, Mau-Mau.

PETE: This chick is going through some weird changes.

MERIDIAN: That's understandable. We all are.

JIMMY: Well, we'll see you sometime tomorrow. It promises to be a kind of *active* day.

MERIDIAN: Yes, we've got some active days ahead of us. You all better get some sleep.

JUANITA: How're you getting home, Jimmy?

JIMMY: Pete's driving us all home.

JUANITA: And then—are you going to drive all the way to your house alone, Pete?

PETE: You're jumpy tonight. I'll stay at Lorenzo's house.

LORENZO: You can call your house from there.

MOTHER HENRY: You get some sleep, too, Meridian, it's past three o'clock in the morning. Don't you stay over here much longer.

MERIDIAN: No, I won't. Good night, all.

MOTHER HENRY: Good night, children. See you in the morning, God willing.

(*They exit. Meridian walks to the pulpit, puts his hand on the Bible. Parnell enters.*)

PARNELL: I hear it was real bad tonight.

MERIDIAN: Not as bad as it's going to get. Maybe I was wrong not to let the people arm.

PARNELL: If the Negroes were armed, it's the Negroes who'd be slaughtered. You know that.

37

MERIDIAN: They're slaughtered anyway. And I don't know that. I thought I knew it—but now I'm not so sure.

PARNELL: What's come over you? What's going to happen to the people in this town, this church—if you go to pieces?

MERIDIAN: Maybe they'll find a leader who can lead them someplace.

PARNELL: Somebody with a gun?
*(Meridian is silent.)*
Is that what you mean?

MERIDIAN: I'm a Christian. I've been a Christian all my life, like my Mama and Daddy before me and like their Mama and Daddy before them. Of course, if you go back far enough, you get to a point *before* Christ, if you see what I mean, B.C.—and at that point, I've been thinking, black people weren't raised to turn the other cheek, and in the hope of heaven. No, then they didn't have to take low. Before Christ. They walked around just as good as anybody else, and when they died, they didn't go to heaven, they went to join their ancestors. My son's dead, but he's not gone to join his ancestors. He was a sinner, so he must have gone to hell—if we're going to believe what the Bible says. Is that such an improvement, such a mighty advance over B.C.? I've been thinking, I've had to think—would I have *been* such a Christian if I hadn't been born black? Maybe I *had* to become a Christian in order to have any dignity at all. Since I wasn't a man in men's eyes, then I could be a man in the eyes of God. But that didn't protect my wife. She's dead, too soon, we don't really know how. That didn't protect my son—he's dead, we know how too well. That hasn't changed this town—this town, where you couldn't find a white Christian at high noon on Sunday! The eyes of God—maybe those eyes are blind—I never let myself think of that before.

38

PARNELL: Meridian, you can't be the man who gives the signal for the holocaust.

MERIDIAN: Must I be the man who watches while his people are beaten, chained, starved, clubbed, butchered?

PARNELL: You used to say that your people were all the people in the world—all the people God ever made, or would make. You said your race was the human race.

MERIDIAN: The human race!

PARNELL: I've never seen you like this before. There's something in your tone I've never heard before—rage—maybe hatred—

MERIDIAN: You've heard it before. You just never recognized it before. You've heard it in all those blues and spirituals and gospel songs you claim to love so much.

PARNELL: I was talking about *you*—not your history. I have a history, too. And don't be so sure I've never heard that sound. Maybe I've never heard anything else. Perhaps my life is also hard to bear.

MERIDIAN: I watched you all this week up at the Police Chief's office with me. And you know how to handle him because you're sure you're better than he is. But you both have more in common with each other than either of you have with me. And, for both of you—I watched this, I never watched it before—it was just a black boy that was dead, and that was a problem. He saw the problem one way, you saw it another way. But it wasn't a *man* that was dead, not my *son*—you held yourselves away from *that!*

PARNELL: I may have sounded—cold. It was not because I felt cold. There was no other way to sound, Meridian. I took the only tone which—it seemed to me—could accomplish what we wanted. And I *do* know the Chief of Police better than you —because I'm white. And I can make him listen to me— because I'm white. I don't know if I think I'm so much

39

better than he is. I know what we have done—and do. But you must have mercy on us. We have no other hope.

MERIDIAN: You have never shown us any mercy at all.

PARNELL: Meridian, give me credit for knowing you're in pain. We are two men, two friends—in spite of all that could divide us. We have come too far together, there is too much at stake, for you to become black now, for me to become white. Don't accuse me. Don't accuse me. *I* didn't do it.

MERIDIAN: So was my son—innocent.

PARNELL: Meridian—when I asked for mercy a moment ago—I meant—please—please try to understand that it is not so easy to leap over fences, to give things up—all right, to surrender privilege! But if you were among the privileged you would know what I mean. It's not a matter of trying to hold *on;* the things, the privilege—are part of you, are *who* you are. It's in the *gut.*

MERIDIAN: Then where's the point of this struggle, where's the hope? If Mister Charlie can't change—

PARNELL: Who's Mister Charlie?

MERIDIAN: You're Mister Charlie. *All* white men are Mister Charlie!

PARNELL: You sound more and more like your son, do you know that? A lot of the colored people here didn't approve of him, but he said things they longed to say—said right out loud, for all the world to hear, how much he despised white people!

MERIDIAN: He didn't say things *I* longed to say. Maybe it was because he was my son. I didn't care *what* he felt about white people. I just wanted him to live, to have his own life. There's something you don't understand about being black, Parnell. If you're a black man, with a black son, you have to forget all about white people and concentrate on trying to save your child. That's why I let him stay up North. I was wrong, I failed, I failed. Lyle walked him up the road and killed him.

PARNELL: We don't *know* Lyle killed him. And Lyle denies it.

MERIDIAN: Of course, he denies it—what do you mean, we don't *know* Lyle killed him?

PARNELL: We *don't* know—all we can say is that it looks that way. And circumstantial evidence is a tricky thing.

MERIDIAN: *When* it involves a white man killing a black man—if Lyle didn't kill him, Parnell, who did?

PARNELL: I don't *know*. But we don't know that Lyle did it.

MERIDIAN: Lyle doesn't deny that he killed Old Bill.

PARNELL: No.

MERIDIAN: And we know how Lyle feels about colored people.

PARNELL: Well, yes. From your point of view. But—from another point of view—Lyle hasn't got anything *against* colored people. He just—

MERIDIAN: He just doesn't think they're human.

PARNELL: Well, even *that's* not true. He doesn't think they're *not* human—after all, I know him, he's hot-tempered and he's far from being the brightest man in the world—but he's not mean, he's not cruel. He's a poor white man. The poor whites have been just as victimized in this part of the world as the blacks have ever been!

MERIDIAN: For God's sake spare me the historical view! Lyle's responsible for Richard's death.

PARNELL: But, Meridian, we can't, even in our own minds, *decide* that he's guilty. We have to operate the way justice *always* has to operate and give him the benefit of the doubt.

MERIDIAN: *What* doubt?

PARNELL: Don't you see, Meridian, that now you're operating the way white people in this town operate whenever a colored man's on trial?

MERIDIAN: When was the last time one of us was on *trial* here, Parnell?

PARNELL: That *can't* have anything to do with it, it *can't*. We must forget about all—*all* the past injustice. We have to start from scratch, or do our best to start from scratch. It isn't vengeance we're after. Is it?

MERIDIAN: I don't want vengeance. I don't want to be paid back—anyway, I couldn't be. I just want Lyle to be made to know that what he did was evil. I just want this town to be forced to face the evil that it countenances and to turn from evil and do good. That's why I've stayed in this town so long!

PARNELL: But if Lyle didn't do it? Lyle is a friend of mine—a strange friend, but a friend. I love him. I know how he suffers.

MERIDIAN: *How* does he suffer?

PARNELL: He suffers—from being in the dark—from having things inside him that he can't name and can't face and can't control. He's not a wicked man. I know he's not, I've known him almost all his life! The face he turns to you, Meridian, isn't the face he turns to me.

MERIDIAN: Is the face he turns to you more real than the face he turns to me? *You* go ask him if he killed my son.

PARNELL: They're going to ask him that in court. That's why I fought to bring about this trial. And he'll say no.

MERIDIAN: I don't care what he says in court. You go ask him. If he's your friend, he'll tell you the truth.

PARNELL: No. No, he may not. He's—he's maybe a little afraid of me.

MERIDIAN: If you're *his* friend, you'll know whether he's telling you the truth or not. Go ask him.

PARNELL: I can't do it. I'm his friend. I can't betray him.

MERIDIAN: But you can betray *me*? You *are* a white man, aren't you? Just another white man—after all.

PARNELL: Even if he says yes, it won't make any difference. The jury will never convict him.

MERIDIAN: Is that why you fought to bring about the trial? I don't care what the jury does. I know he won't say yes to them. He won't say yes to me. But he might say yes to you. You say we don't know. Well, I've got a right to know. And I've got the right to ask you to find out—since you're the only man who *can* find out. And *I've* got to find out—whether we've been friends all these years, or whether I've just been your favorite Uncle Tom.

PARNELL: You know better than that.

MERIDIAN: I don't know, Parnell, any longer—any of the things I used to know. Maybe I never knew them. I'm tired. Go home.

PARNELL: You don't trust me anymore, do you, Meridian?

MERIDIAN: Maybe I never trusted you. I don't know. Maybe I never trusted myself. Go home. Leave me alone. I must look back at my record.

PARNELL: Meridian—what you ask—I don't know if I can do it for you.

MERIDIAN: I don't want you to do it for me. I want you to do it for you. Good night.

PARNELL: Good night.
(*Parnell exists. Meridian comes downstage. It is dawn.*)

MERIDIAN: My record! Would God—would *God*—would God I had died for thee—my son, my son!

*Curtain*

END OF ACT ONE

43

: Here you are, gentlemen. I hope you all drink bourbon.

LPH: Listen to her!

ORGE: Ladies! Would you all like to join us in a morning toast to the happy and beloved and loving couple, Mr. and Mrs. Lyle Britten, on the day immediately preceding their first wedding anniversary?

IS: The bridegroom ain't here because he's weary from all his duties, both public and private. Ha-ha! But he's a good man, and he's done a lot for us, and I know you all know what I'm talking about, and I just feel like we should honor him and his lovely young wife. Ladies! Come on, Reverend Phelps says it's all right.

N: Not too much for me, Ralph.

AN: I don't think I've ever had a drink at this hour of a Sunday morning, and in the presence of my pastor!

(*They pour, drink, and sing* "For He's a Jolly Good Fellow.")

: Now you've started her to crying, naturally. Here, honey, you better have a little drink yourself.

u all have been *so* wonderful. I can't imagine how Lyle can go on sleeping. Thank you, Hazel. Here's to all of you! (*Drinks*) Listen. They're singing over there now.

(*They listen.*)

Sometimes they can sound so nice. Used to take my breath away when I was a girl.

What's happened to this town? It was peaceful here, we all got along, we didn't have no trouble.

Oh, we had a little trouble from time to time, but it didn't mount to a hill of beans. Niggers was all right then, you ould always get you a nigger to help you catch a nigger.

That's right. They had their ways, we had ours, and erything went along the way God intended.

48

WHITETOWN: The kitchen of LYLE's house. Sunday morning. Church bells. A group of white people, all ages, men and women.

JO and an older woman, HAZEL, have just taken a cake out of the oven. HAZEL sets it out to cool.

*Act II*

HAZEL: It's a shame—having to rush everything this way. But it can't be helped.

JO: Yes. I'm just so upset. I can't help it. I know it's silly. I know they can't do nothing to Lyle.

HAZEL: Girl, you just put all those negative thoughts right out of your mind. We're going to have your little anniversary celebration *tonight* instead of *tomorrow* night because we have reason to believe that *tomorrow* night your husband might be called away on business. Now, you think about it that way. Don't you go around here with a great long face, trying to demoralize your guests. I won't have it. You too young and pretty for that.

LILLIAN: Hallelujah! I *do* believe that I have finally mastered this recipe.

SUSAN: Oh, good! Let me see.

LILLIAN: I've only tried it once before, and it's real hard. You've got to time it just right.

SUSAN: I have tried it and tried it and it never comes out! But yours is wonderful! We're going to eat tonight, folks!

RALPH: You supposed to be cooking something, too, ain't you?

SUSAN: I'm cooking our contribution later, at our own house. We got enough women here already, messing up Jo's kitchen.

JO: I'm just so glad you all come by I don't know what to do. Just go ahead and mess up that kitchen, I got lots of time to clean it.

ELLIS: Susan's done learned how to cook, huh?

RALPH: Oh, yeah, she's a right fine cook. All you got to do is look at me. I never weighed this much in my life.

ELLIS: Old Lyle's done gained weight in this year, too. Nothing like steady home cooking, I guess, ha-ha! It really don't seem like it was a year ago you two got married. Declare, I

never thought Lyle was going to jump But old Jo, here, she hooked him.

REV. PHELPS: Well, I said the words over th happy man in my life, it was Big Both of them—there was just a light

GEORGE: I'd propose a toast to them, if it wa and if the Reverend wasn't here.

REV. PHELPS: Ain't nothing wrong with matter what the day or hour.

ELLIS: You heard the Reverend! You got can drink to your happiness in, M

JO: I'm pretty sure we do. It's a pity never slept through this much ra

ELLIS: No ma'am, he ain't never be sleeper. Not before he passed us some times together, him ar sense and got married.

GEORGE: Let him sleep easy. He ain

JO: Lyle's always got his eye on the been at that store, night afte plans and taking inventory cause, come fall, he's plan brand new store, just abo place, I guarantee you!

ELLIS: Lyle's just like his Daddy a thing is, well, the sure will do it. Why, Lyle's was drinking and runni too!—until just before th you stories about the them now, on a Sun women!

JO: I've never been scared in this town before—never. They was all like my own people. I never knew of anyone to mistreat a colored person—have you? And they certainly didn't *act* mistreated. But now, when I walk through this town—I'm scared—like I don't know what's going to happen next. How come the colored people to hate us so much, all of a sudden? We *give* them everything they've got!

REVEREND PHELPS: Their minds have been turned. They have turned away from God. They're a simple people—warm-hearted and good-natured. But they are very easily led, and now they are harkening to the counsel of these degenerate Communist race-mixers. And they don't know what terrible harm they can bring on themselves—and on us all.

JO: You can't tell what they're thinking. Why, colored folks you been knowing all your life—you're almost afraid to hire them, almost afraid to *talk* to them—you don't know what they're thinking.

ELLIS: *I* know what they're thinking.

SUSAN: We're not much better off than the Communist countries— that's what Ralph says. *They* live in fear. They don't want us to teach God in our schools—you send your child to school and you don't know *what* kind of Godless atheist is going to be filling the little one's mind with all *kinds* of filth. And he's going to believe it, of course, kids don't know no better. And now they tell us we got to send our kids to *school* with niggers—why, everybody *knows* that ain't going to work, won't nobody get no education, white *or* black. Niggers can't learn like white folks, they ain't got the same *interests*.

ELLIS: They got one interest. And it's just below the belly button.

GEORGE (*Laughs*): You know them yellow niggers? Boy, ain't they the worst kind? There own folks don't want them, don't nobody want them, and you *can't* do nothing with them—

49

you might be able to scare a black nigger, but you can't do nothing with a yellow nigger.

REVEREND PHELPS: That's because he's a mongrel. And a mongrel is the lowest creation in the animal kingdom.

ELLIS: Mrs. Britten, you're married and all the women in this room are married and I know you've seen your husband without no clothes on—but have you seen a nigger without no clothes on? No, I guess you haven't. Well, he ain't like a white man, Mrs. Britten.

GEORGE: That's right.

ELLIS: Mrs. Britten, if you was to be raped by an orang-outang out of the jungle or a *stallion,* couldn't do you no worse than a nigger. You wouldn't be no more good for nobody. I've *seen* it.

GEORGE: That's *right.*

RALPH: That's why we men have got to be so vigilant. I tell you, I have to be away a lot nights, you know—and I bought Susan a gun and I taught her how to use it, too.

SUSAN: And I'm a pretty good shot now, too. Ralph says he's real proud of me.

RALPH: She's just like a pioneer woman.

HAZEL: I'm so glad Esther's not here to see this. She'd die of shame. She was the sweetest colored woman—you remember her. She just about raised us, used to sing us to sleep at night, and she could tell just the most beautiful stories—the kind of stories that could scare you and make you laugh and make you cry, you know? Oh, she was wonderful. I don't remember a cross word or an evil expression all the time she was with us. She was always the same. And I believe she knew more about me than my own mother and father knew. I just told her everything. Then, one of her sons got killed— he went bad, just like this boy they having a funeral for here tonight—and she got sick. I nursed her, I bathed that woman's body with my own hands. And she told me once, she said, "Miss Hazel, you are just like an angel of light." She said, "My own couldn't have done more for me than you have done." She was a wonderful old woman.

JO: I believe I hear Lyle stirring.

SUSAN: Mrs. Britten, somebody else is coming to call on you. My! It's that Parnell James! I wonder if he's sober this morning. He never *looks* sober.

ELLIS: He never acts it, either.

*(Parnell enters.)*

PARNELL: Good morning, good people! Good morning, Reverend Phelps! How good it is to see brethren—and sistren—walking together. Or, in this case, standing together—something like that, anyway; my Bible's a little rusty. Is church over already? Or are you having it here? Good morning, Jo.

JO: Good morning, Parnell. Sit down, I'll pour you a cup of coffee.

GEORGE: You look like you could use it.

REV. PHELPS: We were all just leaving.

PARNELL: Please don't leave on my account, Reverend Phelps. Just go on as you were, praying or singing, just as the spirit may move you. I *would* love that cup of coffee, Jo.

ELLIS: You been up all night?

PARNELL: Is that the way I look? Yes, I *have* been up all night.

ELLIS: Tom-catting around, I'll bet. Getting drunk and fooling with all the women.

PARNELL: Ah, you flatter me. And in games of chance, my friend, you have no future at all. I'm sure you always lose at poker. So *stop betting*. I was not tom-catting, I was at home, working.

51

GEORGE: You been over the way this morning? You been at the nigger funeral?

PARNELL: The funeral takes place this evening. And, yes, I will be there. Would you care to come along? Leaving your baseball bat at home, of course.

JO: We heard the singing—

PARNELL: Darkies are always singing. You people know that. What made you think it was a funeral?

JO: Parnell! You are the limit! Would anybody else like a little more coffee? It's still good and hot.

ELLIS: We heard that a nigger got killed. That's why we thought it was a funeral.

GEORGE: They bury their dead over the way, don't they?

PARNELL: They do when the dogs leave enough to bury, yes.

   (*A pause*)

ELLIS: Dogs?

PARNELL: Yes—you know. Teeth. Barking. Lots of noise.

ELLIS: A lot of people in this town, Parnell, would like to know exactly where you stand, on a lot of things.

PARNELL: That's exactly where I stand. On a lot of things. Why don't you read my paper?

LILLIAN: I wouldn't filthy my hands with that Communist sheet!

PARNELL: Ah? But the father of your faith, the cornerstone of that church of which you are so precious an adornment, was a communist, possibly the first. He may have done some tomcatting. We *know* he did some drinking. And he knew a lot of—loose ladies and drunkards. It's all in the Bible, isn't it, Reverend Phelps?

REV. PHELPS: I won't be drawn into your blasphemous banter. Ellis is only asking what many of us want to know—are you with us or against us? And he's telling you what we all feel.

We've put up with your irresponsibility long enough. We won't tolerate it any longer. Do I make myself clear?

PARNELL: Not at all. If you're threatening me, be specific. First of all, what's this irresponsibility that you won't tolerate? And if you aren't going to tolerate it, what *are* you going to do? Dip me in tar and feathers? Boil me in oil? Castrate me? Burn me? Cover yourselves in white sheets and come and burn crosses in front of my house? Come on, Reverend Phelps, don't stand there with your mouth open, it makes you even more repulsive than you are with it closed, and all your foul, graveyard breath comes rushing out, and it makes me want to vomit. Out with it, boy! What's on your mind?

ELLIS: You got away with a lot of things in this town, Parnell, for a long time, because your father was a big man here.

PARNELL: One at a time. I was addressing your spiritual leader.

SUSAN: He's *worse* than a nigger.

PARNELL: I take that as a compliment. I'm sure no man will ever say as much for you. Reverend Phelps?

REV. PHELPS: I think I speak for us all—for *myself* and for us all, when I say that our situation down here has become much too serious for flippancy and cynicism. When things were more in order here, we didn't really mind your attitude, and your paper didn't matter to us, we never read it, anyway.

ELLIS: We knew you were just a spoiled rich boy, with too much time on his hands that he didn't know what to do with.

REV. PHELPS: And so you started this paper and tried to make yourself interesting with all these subversive attitudes. I honestly thought that you would grow out of it.

GEORGE: Or go North.

REV. PHELPS: I know these attitudes were not your father's attitudes, or your mother's. I was very often invited to your home when they were alive—

53

PARNELL: How well I remember! What attitudes are you speaking of?

HAZEL: Race-mixing!

PARNELL: *Race-mixing!* Ladies and gentlemen, do you think anybody gives a good goddamn who you sleep with? You can go down to the swamps and couple with the snakes, for all I care, or for all anybody else cares. You may find that the snakes don't want you, but that's a problem for you and the snakes to work out, and it might prove astonishingly simple—the working out of the problem, I mean. I've never said a word about race-mixing. I've talked about social justice.

LILLIAN: That sounds Communistic to me!

PARNELL: It means that if I have a hundred dollars, and I'm black, and you have a hundred dollars, and you're white, I should be able to get as much value for *my* hundred dollars—my black hundred dollars—as you get for your *white* hundred dollars. It also means that I should have an equal opportunity to *earn* that hundred dollars—

ELLIS: Niggers can get work just as well as a white man can. Hell, *some* niggers make *more* money than me.

PARNELL: Some niggers are smarter than you, Ellis. Much smarter. And much nicer. And niggers *can't* get work just as well as a white man can, and you know it.

ELLIS: What's stopping them? They got hands.

PARNELL: Ellis, you don't really work with your *hands*—you're a salesman in a shoe store. And your boss wouldn't give that job to a nigger.

GEORGE: Well, goddammit, white men come before niggers! They *got* to!

PARNELL: Why?

(*Lyle enters.*)

LYLE: What's all this commotion going on in my house?

JO: Oh, Lyle, good morning! Some folks just dropped in to see you.

LYLE: It sounded like they was about to come to blows. Good morning, Reverend Phelps, I'm glad to see you here. I'm sorry I wasn't up, but I guess my wife might have told you, I've not been sleeping well nights. When I *do* go to sleep, she just lets me sleep on.

REV. PHELPS: Don't you apologize, son—we understand. We only came by to let you know that we're with you and every white person in this town is with you.

JO: Isn't that nice of them, Lyle? They've been here quite a spell, and we've had *such* a nice time.

LYLE: Well, that *is* mighty nice of you, Reverend, and all of you—hey there, Ellis! Old George! And Ralph and Susan—how's married life suit you? Guess it suits you all right, ain't nobody seen you in months, ha-ha! Mrs. Proctor, Mrs. Barker, how you all? Hey! Old Parnell! What you doing up so early?

PARNELL: I was on my way to church, but they seemed to be having the meeting here. So I joined the worshippers.

LYLE: On your way to church, that's a good one. Bet you ain't been to bed yet.

PARNELL: No, I haven't.

LYLE: You folks don't mind if I have a little breakfast? Jo, bring me something to eat! Susan, you look mighty plump and rosy, you ain't keeping no secrets from us, are you?

SUSAN: I don't think so, Lyle.

LYLE: I don't know, you got that look—like a real ripe peach, just right for eating. You ain't been slack in your duty, have you, Ralph? Look at the way she's blushing! I guess you all right, boy.

55

ELLIS: You know what time they coming for you tomorrow?

LYLE: Sometime in the morning, I reckon. I don't know.

REV. PHELPS: I saw the Chief of Police the other day. He really doesn't want to do it, but his hands are tied. It's orders from higher up, from the North.

LYLE: Shoot, I know old Frank don't want to arrest me. I understand. I ain't worried. I know the people in this town is with me. I got nothing to worry about.

ELLIS: They trying to force us to put niggers on the jury—that's what I hear. Claim it won't be a fair trial if we don't.

HAZEL: Did you *ever* hear anything like that in your *life?*

LYLE: Where they going to find the niggers?

ELLIS: Oh, I bet your buddy, Parnell, has got that all figured out.

LYLE: How about it, Parnell? You going to find some niggers for them to put on that jury?

PARNELL: It's not up to me. But I might recommend a couple.

GEORGE: And how they going to get to court? You going to protect them?

PARNELL: The police will protect them. Or the State troopers—

GEORGE: That's a good one!

PARNELL: Or Federal marshals.

GEORGE: Look here, you really think there should be niggers on that jury?

PARNELL: Of course I do, and so would you, if you had any sense. For one thing, they're forty-four percent of the population of this town.

ELLIS: But they don't vote. Not most of them.

PARNELL: Well. That's also a matter of interest to the Federal government. Why *don't* they vote? They got hands.

ELLIS: You claim Lyle's your buddy—

PARNELL: Lyle *is* my buddy. That's why I want him to have a fair trial.

HAZEL: I can't listen to no more of this, I'm sorry, I just can't. Honey, I'll see you all tonight, you hear?

REV. PHELPS: We're all going to go now. We just wanted to see how you were, and let you know that you could count on us.

LYLE: I sure appreciate it, Reverend, believe me, I do. You make me feel much better. Even if a man knows he ain't done no wrong, still, it's a kind of troublesome spot to be in. Wasn't for my good Jo, here, I don't know what I'd do. Good morning, Mrs. Barker. Mrs. Proctor. So long, George, it's been good to see you. Ralph, you take good care of Susan, you hear? And name the first one after me—you might have to bring it on up to the jail house so I can see it.

SUSAN: Don't think like that. Everything's going to be all right.

LYLE: You're sure?

SUSAN: I guarantee it. Why they couldn't—*couldn't*—do anything to you!

LYLE: Then I believe it. I believe *you*.

SUSAN: You keep right on believing.

ELLIS: Remember what we said, Parnell.

PARNELL: So long, Ellis. See you next Halloween.

LYLE: Let's get together, boy, soon as this mess is over.

ELLIS: You bet. This mess is just about over now—we ain't going to let them prolong it. And I know just the thing'll knock all this clear out of your mind, this, and everything else, ha-ha! Bye-bye, Mrs. Britten.

JO: Goodbye. And thanks for coming!

(*Hazel, Lillian, Susan, Ralph, Ellis, Reverend Phelps and George exit.*)

LYLE: They're nice people.

JO: Yes. They are.

PARNELL: They certainly think a lot of you.

LYLE: You ain't jealous, are you, boy? No. We've all had the same kind of trouble—it's the kind of trouble you wouldn't know about, Parnell, because you've never had to worry about making your living. But me! I been doing hard work from the time I was a puppy. Like my Mama and Daddy before me, God rest their souls, and their Mama and Daddy before them. They wore themselves out on the land—the land never give them nothing. Nothing but an empty belly and some skinny kids. I'm the only one growed up to be a man. That's because I take after my Daddy—he was skinny as a piece of wire, but he was hard as any rock. And stubborn! Lord, you ain't never seen nobody so stubborn. He should have been born sooner. Had he been born sooner, when this was still a free country, and a man could really *make* some money, I'd have been born rich as you, Parnell, maybe even richer. I tell you—the old man struggled. He worked harder than any nigger. But he left me this store.

JO: You reckon we going to be able to leave it to the little one?

LYLE: We're going to leave him more than that. That little one ain't going to have nothing to worry about. I'm going to leave him as rich as old Parnell here, and he's going to be educated, too, better than his Daddy; better, even, than Parnell!

PARNELL: You going to send him to school in Switzerland?

LYLE: *You* went there for a while, didn't you?

JO: That's where Parnell picked up all his wild ideas.

PARNELL: Yes. Be careful. There were a couple of African princes studying in the school I went to—they did a lot more studying than I did, I must say.

58

LYLE: African princes, huh? What were they like? Big and black, I bet, elephant tusks hanging around their necks.

PARNELL: Some of them wore a little ivory, on a chain—silver chain. They were like everybody else. Maybe they thought they were a little *better* than most of us—the Swiss girls certainly thought so.

LYLE: The *Swiss* girls? You mean they didn't have no women of their own?

PARNELL: Lots of them. Swiss women, Danish women, English women, French women, Finns, Russians, even a couple of Americans.

JO: I don't believe you. Or else they was just trying to act like foreigners. I can't stand people who try to act like something they're not.

PARNELL: They were just trying to act like women—poor things. And the Africans were men, no one had ever told them that they weren't.

LYLE: You mean there weren't no African women around at *all?* Weren't the Swiss people kind of upset at having all these niggers around with no women?

PARNELL: They didn't seem to be upset. They seemed delighted. The niggers had an awful lot of money. And there weren't many African girls around because African girls aren't educated the way American girls are.

JO: The American girls didn't *mind* going out with the Africans?

PARNELL: Not at all. It appears that the Africans were excellent dancers.

LYLE: I won't never send no daughter of mine to Switzerland.

PARNELL: Well, what about your son? *He* might grow fond of some little African princess.

LYLE: Well, that's different. I don't care about that, long as he leaves her over there.

JO: It's *not* different—how can you say that? White men ain't got no more business fooling around with black women than—

LYLE: Girl, will you stop getting yourself into an uproar? Men is different from women—they ain't as delicate. Man can do a lot of things a woman can't do, you know that.

PARNELL: You've heard the expression, sowing wild oats? Well, all the men we know sowed a lot of wild oats before they finally settled down and got married.

LYLE: That's right. Men *have* to do it. They ain't like women. Parnell is *still* sowing his wild oats—I sowed mine.

JO: And a woman that wants to be a decent woman just has to —*wait*—until the men get tired of going to bed with—harlots! —and decide to settle down?

PARNELL: Well, it sounds very unjust, I know, but that's the way it's always been. I *suppose* the decent women were wait-ing—though nobody seems to know *exactly* how they spent the time.

JO: Parnell!

PARNELL: Well, there *are* some who waited too long.

JO: Men ought to be ashamed. How can you blame a woman if she—goes wrong? If a decent woman can't find a decent man—why—it must happen all the time—they get tired of waiting.

LYLE: Not if they been raised right, no sir, that's what my Daddy said, and I've never known it to fail. And look at you—*you* didn't get tired of waiting. Ain't nobody in this town ever been able to say a word against you. Man, I was so scared when I finally asked this girl to marry me. I was afraid she'd turn me out of the house. Because I had been pretty wild. Parnell can tell you.

JO: I had heard.

LYLE: But she didn't. I looked at her, it seemed almost like it was
the first time—you know, the first time you really *look* at a
woman?—and I thought, I'll be damned if I don't believe I
can make it with her. I believe I can. And she looked at me
like she loved me. It was in her eyes. And it was just like
somebody had lifted a great big load off my heart.

JO: You shouldn't be saying these things in front of Parnell.

LYLE: Why not? I ain't got no secrets from Parnell—he knows
about men and women. Look at her blush! Like I told you.
Women is more delicate than men.
*(He touches her face lightly.)*
I know you kind of upset, sugar. But don't you be nervous.
Everything's going to be all right, and we're going to be
happy again, you'll see.

JO: I hope so, Lyle.

LYLE: I'm going to take me a bath and put some clothes on. Parnell,
you sit right there, you hear? I won't be but a minute.
*(Exits.)*

JO: What a funny man he is! It don't do no good at all to get mad
at him, you might as well get mad at that baby in there.
Parnell? Can I ask you something?

PARNELL: Certainly.

JO: Is it true that Lyle has no secrets from you?

PARNELL: He said that *neither* of you had any secrets from me.

JO: Oh, don't play. Lyle don't know a thing about women—what
they're really like, to themselves. Men don't know. But I
want to ask you a serious question. Will you answer it?

PARNELL: If I can.

JO: That means you won't answer it. But I'll ask it, anyway. Parnell—was Lyle—is it true what people said? That he was
having an affair with Old Bill's wife and that's why he shot
Old Bill?

PARNELL: Why are you asking me that?

JO: Because I have to know! It's true, isn't it? He had an affair with Old Bill's wife—and he had affairs with lots of colored women in this town. It's *true*. Isn't it?

PARNELL: What does it matter who he slept with before he married you, Jo? I know he had a—lot of prostitutes. Maybe some of them were colored. When he was drunk, he wouldn't have been particular.

JO: He's never talked to you about it?

PARNELL: Why would he?

JO: Men talk about things like that.

PARNELL: Men often joke about things like that. But, Jo—what one man tells another man, his friend—can't be told to women.

JO: Men certainly stick together. I wish women did. All right. You can't talk about Lyle. But tell me this. Have *you* ever had an affair with a colored girl? I don't mean a—a *night*. I mean, did she mean something to you, did you like her, did you— love her? Could you have married her—I mean, just like you would marry a white woman?

PARNELL: Jo—

JO: Oh! Tell me the truth, Parnell!

PARNELL: I loved a colored girl, yes. I think I loved her. But I was only eighteen and she was only seventeen. I was still a virgin. I don't know if she was, but I think she was. A lot of the other kids in school used to drive over to niggertown at night to try and find black women. Sometimes they bought them, sometimes they frightened them, sometimes they raped them. And they were proud of it, they talked about it all the time. I couldn't do that. Those kids made me ashamed of my own body, ashamed of everything I felt, ashamed of being white—

62

JO: Ashamed of being white.

PARNELL: Yes.

JO: How did you meet—this colored girl?

PARNELL: Her mother worked for us. She used to come, sometimes, to pick up her mother. Sometimes she had to wait. I came in once and found her in the library, she was reading Stendhal. *The Red and The Black.* I had just read it and we talked about it. She was funny—very bright and solemn and very proud—and she was *scared,* scared of me, but much too proud to show it. Oh, she was funny. But she was bright.

JO: What did she look like?

PARNELL: She was the color of gingerbread when it's just come out of the oven. I used to call her Ginger—later. Her name was really Pearl. She had black hair, very black, kind of short, and she dressed it very carefully. Later, I used to tease her about the way she took care of her hair. There's a girl in this town now who reminds me of her. Oh, I loved her!

JO: What happened?

PARNELL: I used to look at her, the way she moved, so beautiful and free, and I'd wonder if at night, when she might be on her way home from someplace, any of those boys at school had said ugly things to her. And then I thought that I wasn't any better than they were, because I thought my own thoughts were pretty awful. And I wondered what she thought of me. But I didn't dare to ask. I got so I could hardly think of anyone but her. I got sick wanting to take her in my arms, to take her in my arms and love her and protect her from all those other people who wanted to destroy her. She wrote a little poetry, sometimes she'd show it to me, but she really wanted to be a painter.

JO: What happened?

PARNELL: Nothing happened. We got so we told each other everything. She was going to be a painter, I was going to be a

63

writer. It was our secret. Nobody in the world knew about her *inside,* what she was like, and how she dreamed, but me. And nobody in the world knew about *me* inside, what I wanted, and how I dreamed, but her. But we couldn't look ahead, we didn't dare. We talked about going North, but I was still in school, and she was still in school. We couldn't be seen anywhere together—it would have given her too bad a name. I used to see her sometimes in the movies, with various colored boys. She didn't seem to have any special one. They'd be sitting in the balcony, in the colored section, and I'd be sitting downstairs in the white section. She couldn't come down to me, I couldn't go up to her. We'd meet some nights, late, out in the country, but—I didn't want to take her in the bushes, and I couldn't take her any-where else. One day we were sitting in the library, we were kissing, and her mother came in. That was the day I found out how much black people can hate white people.

JO: What did her mother do?

PARNELL: She didn't say a word. She just looked at me. She just looked at me. I could see what was happening in her mind. She knew that there wasn't any point in complaining to my mother or my father. It would just make her daughter look bad. She didn't dare tell her husband. If he tried to do any-thing, he'd be killed. There wasn't anything she could do about me. I was just another horny white kid trying to get into a black girl's pants. She looked at me as though she were wishing with all her heart that she could raise her hand and wipe me off the face of the earth. I'll never forget that look. I still see it. She walked over to Pearl and I thought she was going to slap her. But she didn't. She took her by the hand, very sadly, and all she said was, "I'm ready to go now. Come on." And she took Pearl out of the room.

JO: Did you ever see her again?

PARNELL: No. Her mother sent her away.

JO: But you forgot her? You must have had lots of other girls right quick, right after that.

PARNELL: I never forgot her.

JO: Do you think of her—even when you're with Loretta?

PARNELL: Not all of the time, Jo. But some of the time—yes.

JO: And if you found her again?

PARNELL: If I found her again—yes, I'd marry her. I'd give her the children I've always wanted to have.

JO: Oh, Parnell! If you felt that way about her, if you've felt it all this time!

PARNELL: Yes. I know. I'm a renegade white man.

JO: Then Lyle could have felt that way about Old Bill's wife—about Willa Mae. I know that's not the way he feels about me. And if he felt that way—he could have shot Old Bill—to keep him quiet!

PARNELL: Jo!

JO: Yes! And if he could have shot Old Bill to keep him quiet—he could have killed that boy. He could have killed that boy. And if he did—well—that *is* murder, isn't it? It's just nothing but murder, even if the boy *was* black. Oh, Parnell! Parnell!

PARNELL: Jo, please. Please, Jo. Be quiet.

LYLE (*Off*): What's all that racket in there?

PARNELL: I'm telling your wife the story of my life.

LYLE (*Off*): Sounds pretty goddamn active.

PARNELL: You've never asked him, have you, Jo?

JO: No. No. No.

PARNELL: Well, *I* asked him—

JO: When?

65

PARNELL: Well, I didn't really *ask* him. But he said he didn't do it, that it wasn't true. You heard him. He wouldn't lie to me.

JO: No. He wouldn't lie to you. They say some of the niggers have guns—did you hear that?

PARNELL: Yes. I've heard it. But it's not true.

JO: *They* wouldn't lie to you, either? I've just had too much time to worry, I guess—brood and worry. Lyle's away so often nights —he spends so much time at that store. I don't know what he does there. And when he comes home, he's just dead— and he drops right off to sleep.

(*Lyle enters, carrying the child.*)

Hi, honey. What a transformation. You look like you used to look when you come courting.

LYLE: I sure didn't come courting carrying no baby. He was awake, just singing away, and carrying on with his toes. He acts like he thinks he's got a whole lot of candy attached to the end of his legs. Here. It's about time for him to eat, ain't it? How come you looking at me like that? Why you being so nice to me, all of a sudden?

PARNELL: I've been lecturing her on the duties of a wife.

LYLE: That so? Well, come on, boy, let's you and me walk down the road a piece. Believe I'll buy you a drink. You ain't ashamed to be seen with me, I hope?

PARNELL: No, I'm not ashamed to be seen with you.

JO: You going to be home for supper?

LYLE: Yeah, sugar. Come on, Parnell.

JO: You come, too, Parnell, you and Loretta, if you're free. We'd love to have you.

PARNELL: We'll try to make it. So long, Jo.

JO: So long.

*(They exit. Jo walks to the window. Turns back into the room, smiles down at the baby. Sings.)*

> Hush, little baby, don't say a word,
> Mama's going to buy you a mocking bird—

But you don't want no mocking bird right now, do you? I know what you want. You want something to eat. All right, Mama's going to feed you.

*(Sits, slowly begins to unbutton her blouse. Sings.)*

> If that mocking bird don't sing,
> Mama's going to buy you a diamond ring.

*(LYLE'S STORE: Early evening. Both Lyle and Parnell are a little drunk.)*

LYLE: Didn't you ever get like that? Sure, you must have got like that sometimes—just restless! You got everything you need and you can't complain about nothing—and yet, look like, you just can't be satisfied. Didn't you ever get like that? I swear, men is mighty strange! I'm kind of restless now.

PARNELL: What's the matter with you? You worried about the trial?

LYLE: No, I ain't worried about the trial. I ain't even mad at you, Parnell. Some folks think I should be, but I ain't mad at you. They don't know you like I know you. I ain't fooled by all your wild ideas. We both white and we both from around here, and we been buddies all our lives. That's all that counts. I know you ain't going to let nothing happen to me.

PARNELL: That's good to hear.

LYLE: After all the trouble started in this town—but before that crazy boy got himself killed, soon after he got here and started raising all that hell—I started thinking about her, about Willa Mae, more and more and more. She was too young for him. Old Bill, he was sixty if he was a day, he wasn't doing her no good. Yet and still, the first time I took Willa Mae, I had to fight her. I swear I did. Maybe she was

67

frightened. But I never had to fight her again. No. It was good, boy, let me tell you, and she liked it as much as me. Hey! You still with me?

PARNELL: I'm still with you. Go on.

LYLE: What's the last thing I said?

PARNELL: That she liked it as much as you—which I find hard to believe.

LYLE: Ha-ha! I'm telling you. I never had it for nobody bad as I had it for her.

PARNELL: When did Old Bill find out?

LYLE: Old Bill? He wouldn't never have thought nothing if people hadn't started poisoning his mind. People started talking just because my Daddy wasn't well and she was up at the house so much because somebody had to look after him. First they said she was carrying on with *him*. Hell, my Daddy would sure have been willing, but he was far from able. He was really wore out by that time and he just wanted rest. Then people started to saying that it was me.

PARNELL: Old Bill ever talk to you about it?

LYLE: How was he going to talk to me about it? Hell, we was right good friends. Many's the time I helped Old Bill out when his cash was low. I used to load Willa Mae up with things from the kitchen just to make sure they didn't go hungry.

PARNELL: Old Bill never mentioned it to you? Never? He never gave you any reason to think he knew about it?

LYLE: Well, I don't know what was going on in his *mind*, Parnell. You can't never see what's in anybody else's *mind*—you know that. He didn't *act* no different. Hell, like I say, she was young enough to be his granddaughter damn near, so I figured he thought it might be a pretty good arrangement— me doing *his* work, ha-ha! because *he* damn sure couldn't do it no more, and helping him to stay alive.

PARNELL: Then why was he so mad at you the last time you saw him?

LYLE: Like I said, he accused me of cheating him. And I ain't never cheated a black man in my life. I hate to say it, because we've always been good friends, but sometimes I think it might have been Joel—Papa D.—who told him that. Old Bill wasn't too good at figuring.

PARNELL: Why would Papa D. tell him a thing like that?

LYLE: I think he might have been a little jealous.

PARNELL: Jealous? You mean, of you and Willa Mae?

LYLE: Yeah. He ain't really an old man, you know. But I'm sure he didn't mean—for things to turn out like they did. (*A pause*) I can still see him—the way he looked when he come into this store.

PARNELL: The way *who* looked when he came into this store?

LYLE: Why—Old Bill. He looked crazy. Like he wanted to kill me. He *did* want to kill me. Crazy nigger.

PARNELL: I thought you meant the other one. But the other one didn't die in the store.

LYLE: Old Bill didn't die in the store. He died over yonder, in the road.

PARNELL: I thought you were talking about Richard Henry.

LYLE: That crazy boy. Yeah, he come in here. I don't know what was the matter with him, he hadn't seen me but one time in his life before. And I treated him like—like I would have treated *any* man.

PARNELL: I heard about it. It was in Papa D.'s joint. He was surrounded by niggers—or *you* were—

LYLE: He was dancing with one of them crazy young ones—the real pretty nigger girl—what's her name?

PARNELL: Juanita.

LYLE: That's the one. (*Juke box music, soft. Voices. Laughter*) Yeah. He looked at me like he wanted to kill me. And he insulted my wife. And I hadn't never done him no harm. (*As above, a little stronger*) But I been thinking about it. And you know what I think? Hey! You gone to sleep?

PARNELL: No. I'm thinking.

LYLE: What you thinking about?

PARNELL: Us. You and me.

LYLE: And what do you think about us—you and me? What's the point of thinking about us, anyway? We've been buddies all our lives—we can't stop being buddies now.

PARNELL: That's right, buddy. What were you about to say?

LYLE: Oh. I think a lot of the niggers in this town, especially the young ones, is turned bad. And I believe they was egging him on.

(*A pause. The music stops.*)

He come in here one Monday afternoon. Everybody heard about it, it was all over this town quicker'n a jack-rabbit gets his nuts off. You just missed it. You'd just walked out of here.

(*Lyle rises, walks to the doors and opens them. Sunlight fills the room. He slams the screen doors shut; we see the road.*)

JO (*Off*): Lyle, you want to help me bring this baby carriage inside? It's getting kind of hot out here now.

PARNELL: Let *me*.

(*Lyle and Parnell bring in the baby carriage. Jo enters.*)

JO: My, it's hot! Wish we'd gone for a ride or something. Declare to goodness, we ain't got no reason to be sitting around this store. Ain't nobody coming in here—not to *buy* anything, anyway.

PARNELL: I'll buy some bubble gum.

70

JO: You know you don't chew bubble gum.

PARNELL: Well, then, I'll buy some cigarettes.

JO: Two cartons, or three? It's all right, Parnell, the Britten family's going to make it somehow.

LYLE: Couple of niggers coming down the road. Maybe they'll drop in for a Coke.

(*Exits, into back of store.*)

JO: Why, no, they won't. Our Cokes is *poisoned.* I get up every morning before daybreak and drop the arsenic in myself.

PARNELL: Well, then, I won't have a Coke. See you, Jo. So long, Lyle!

LYLE (*Off*): Be seeing you!

(*Parnell exits. Silence for a few seconds. Then we hear Lyle hammering in the back. Jo picks up a magazine, begins to read. Voices. Richard and Lorenzo appear in the road.*)

RICHARD: Hey, you want a Coke? I'm thirsty.

LORENZO: Let's go on a little further.

RICHARD: Man, we been walking for *days,* my mouth is as dry as that damn dusty road. Come on, have a Coke with me, won't take but a minute.

LORENZO: We don't trade in there. Come on—

RICHARD: Oh! Is this the place? Hell, I'd like to get another look at the peckerwood, ain't going to give him but a dime. I want to get his face fixed in my *mind,* so there won't be no time wasted when the time comes, you dig? (*Enters the store*) Hey, Mrs. Ofay Ednolbay Ydalay! you got any Coca Cola for sale? (For Blonde Lady)

JO: What?

RICHARD: Coke! Me and my man been toting barges and lifting bales, that's right, we been slaving, and we need a little cool. Liquid. Refreshment. Yeah, and you can take that hammer, too.

71

JO: Boy, what do you want?

RICHARD: A Coca Cola, ma'am. Please ma'am.

JO: They right in the box there.

RICHARD: Thank you kindly. (*Takes two Cokes, opens them*) Oh, this is fine, *fine*. Did you put them in this box with your own little dainty dish-pan hands? Sure makes them taste *sweet*.

JO: Are you talking to me?

RICHARD: No ma'am, just feel like talking to myself from time to time, makes the time pass faster. (*At screen door*) Hey, Lorenz, I got you a Coke.

LORENZO: I don't want it. Come on out of there.

JO: That will be twenty cents.

RICHARD: *Twenty* cents? All right. Don't you know how to say please? All the women *I* know say please—of course, they ain't as pretty as you. I ain't got twenty cents, ma'am. All I got is—twenty dollars!

JO: You ain't got nothing smaller?

RICHARD: No ma'am. You see, I don't never carry on me more cash than I can afford to *lose*.

JO: Lyle! (*Lyle enters, carrying the hammer*) You got any change?

LYLE: Change for a twenty? No, you know I ain't got it.

RICHARD: You all got this big, fine store and all—and you ain't got change for *twenty* dollars?

LYLE: It's early in the day, boy.

RICHARD: It ain't that early. I thought white folks was rich at *every* hour of the day.

LYLE: Now, if you looking for trouble, you just might get it. That boy outside—ain't he got twenty cents?

72

RICHARD: That boy outside is about twenty-four years old, and he ain't got twenty cents. Ain't no need to ask him.

LYLE (*At the door*): Boy! You got twenty cents?

LORENZO: Come on out of there, Richard! I'm tired of hanging around here!

LYLE: Boy, didn't you hear what I asked you?

LORENZO: Mister Britten, I ain't *in* the store, and I ain't *bought* nothing in the store, and so I ain't *got* to tell you whether or not I got twenty cents!

RICHARD: Maybe your wife could run home and get some change. You *got* some change at home, I know. Don't you?

LYLE: I don't stand for nobody to talk about my wife.

RICHARD: I only said you was a lucky man to have so fine a *wife.* I said maybe she could run *home* and look and see if there was any change—in the *home.*

LYLE: I seen you before some place. You that crazy nigger. You ain't from around here.

RICHARD: You *know* you seen me. And you remember where. And when. I was born right here, in this town. I'm Reverend Meridian Henry's son.

LYLE: You say that like you thought your Daddy's name was some kind of protection. He ain't no protection against *me*—him, nor that boy outside, neither.

RICHARD: I don't need no protection, do I? Not in my own home town, in the good old USA. I just dropped by to sip on a Coke in a simple country store—and come to find out the joker ain't got enough bread to change twenty dollars. Stud ain't got *nothing*—you people been spoofing the public, man.

LYLE: You put them Cokes down and get out of here.

RICHARD: I ain't finished yet. And I ain't changed my bill yet.

73

LYLE: Well, I ain't going to change that bill, and you ain't going to finish them Cokes. You get your black ass out of here—go on! If you got any sense, you'll get your black ass out of this town.

RICHARD: You don't own this town, you white mother-fucker. You don't *even* own twenty dollars. Don't you raise that hammer. I'll take it and beat your skull to jelly.

JO: Lyle! Don't you fight that boy! He's crazy! I'm going to call the Sheriff! (*Starts toward the back, returns to counter*) The baby! Lyle! Watch out for the baby!

RICHARD: A baby, huh? How many times did you have to try for it, you no-good, ball-less peckerwood? I'm surprised you could even get it up—look at the way you sweating now.

(*Lyle raises the hammer. Richard grabs his arm, forcing it back. They struggle.*)

JO: Lyle! The baby!

LORENZO: Richard!

(*He comes into the store.*)

JO: Please get that boy out of here, get that boy out of here—he's going to get himself killed.

(*Richard knocks the hammer from Lyle's hand, and knocks Lyle down. The hammer spins across the room. Lorenzo picks it up.*)

LORENZO: I don't think your husband's going to kill no more black men. Not today, Mrs. Britten. Come on, Richard. Let's go.

(*Lyle looks up at them.*)

LYLE: It took two of you. Remember that.

LORENZO: I didn't lay a hand on you, Mister Britten. You just ain't no match for—a *boy*. Not without your gun you ain't. Come on, Richard.

JO: You'll go to jail for this! You'll go to jail! For years!

LORENZO: We've been in jail for years. I'll leave your hammer over at Papa D.'s joint—don't look like you're going to be doing no more work today.

RICHARD (*Laughs*): Look at the mighty peckerwood! On his *ass*, baby—and his woman watching! Now, who you think is the better man? Ha-ha! The master race! You let me in that tired white chick's drawers, she'll know who's the master! Ha-ha-ha!
(*Exits. Richard's laughter continues in the dark. Lyle and Parnell as before.*)

LYLE: Niggers was laughing at me for days. Everywhere I went.

PARNELL: You never did call the Sheriff.

LYLE: No.
(*Parnell fills their glasses. We hear singing.*)

PARNELL: It's almost time for his funeral.

LYLE: And may every nigger like that nigger end like that nigger—face down in the weeds!
(*A pause.*)

PARNELL: Was he lying face down?

LYLE: Hell, yeah, he was face down. Said so in the papers.

PARNELL: Is that what the papers said? I don't remember.

LYLE: Yeah, that's what the papers said.

PARNELL: I guess they had to turn him over—to make sure it was him.

LYLE: I reckon. (*Laughs*) Yeah. I reckon.

PARNELL: You and me are buddies, huh?

LYLE: *Yeah,* we're buddies—to the end!

PARNELL: I always wondered why you wanted to be my buddy. A lot of poor guys hate rich guys. I always wondered why you weren't like that.

75

LYLE: I ain't like that. Hell, Parnell, you're smarter than me. I know it. I used to wonder what made you smarter than me. I got to be your buddy so I could find out. Because, hell, you didn't seem so different in *other* ways—in spite of all your *ideas.* Two things we always had in common—liquor and poon-tang. We couldn't get enough of neither one. Of course, your liquor might have been a little better. But I doubt if the other could have been any better!

PARNELL: Did you find out what made me smarter?

LYLE: Yeah. You richer!

PARNELL: I'm richer! That's all you got to tell me—about Richard Henry?

LYLE: Ain't nothing more to tell. Wait till after the trial. You won't have to ask me no more questions then!

PARNELL: I've got to get to the funeral.

LYLE: Don't run off. Don't leave me here alone.

PARNELL: You're supposed to be home for supper.

LYLE: Supper can wait. Have another drink with me—be my buddy. Don't leave me here alone. Listen to them! Singing and praying! Singing and praying and laughing behind a man's back!

(*The singing continues in the dark.* BLACKTOWN: *The church, packed. Meridian in the pulpit, the bier just below him.*)

MERIDIAN: My heart is heavier tonight than it has ever been before. I raise my voice to you tonight out of a sorrow and a wonder I have never felt before. Not only I, my Lord, am in this case. Everyone under the sound of my voice, and many more souls than that, feel as I feel, and tremble as I tremble, and bleed as I bleed. It is not that the days are dark—we have known dark days. It is not only that the blood runs down and no man helps us; it is not only that our children are destroyed before our eyes. It is not only that our lives, from day to day and every hour of each day, are menaced by the people among whom you have set us down. We have borne all these things, my Lord, and we have done what the prophets of old could not do, we have sung the Lord's song in a strange land. In a strange land! What was the sin committed by our forefathers in the time that has vanished on the other side of the flood, which has had to be expiated by chains, by the lash, by hunger and thirst, by slaughter, by fire, by the rope, by the knife, and for so many generations, on these wild shores, in this strange land? Our offense must have been mighty, our crime immeasurable. But it is not the past which makes our hearts so heavy. It is the present. Lord, where is our hope? Who, or what, shall touch the hearts of this headlong and unthinking people and turn them back from destruction? When will they hear the words of John? *I know thy works, that thou art neither cold nor hot: I would that thou wert cold or hot. So, then because thou art lukewarm and neither cold nor hot, I will spew thee out of my mouth. Because thou sayest, I am rich and increased with goods, and have need of nothing; and knowest not that thou art wretched and miserable and poor and blind and naked.* Now, when the children come, my Lord, and ask which road to follow, my tongue stammers and my heart fails. I will not abandon the land—this strange land, which is my home. But can I ask the children forever to sustain the cruelty inflicted on them by those who have been their masters, and who are now, in very truth, their kinfolk, their brothers and their sisters and their parents? What hope is there for a people who deny their deeds and disown their kinsmen and who do so in the name of purity and love, in the name of Jesus Christ? What a light, my Lord, is needed to conquer so mighty a darkness! This darkness rules in us, and grows, in black and white alike. I have set my face against the darkness, I will not let it conquer me, even though it will, I know, one day, destroy this body. But, my Lord, what of the children? What shall I tell the children? I must be with you, Lord, like Jacob, and wrestle with you until the light appears—I will not let you go until you give me a sign! A sign that in the terrible Sahara of our time a fountain may spring, the fountain of a true morality, and bring us closer, oh, my Lord, to that peace on earth desired by so few throughout so many ages. Let not our suffering endure forever. Teach us to trust the great gift of life and learn to love one another and dare to walk the earth like men. Amen.

MOTHER HENRY: Let's file up, children, and say goodbye.

(*Song*: "Great Getting-Up Morning." *Meridian steps down from the pulpit. Meridian, Lorenzo, Jimmy and Pete shoulder the bier. A dishevelled Parnell enters. The Congregation and the Pallbearers file past him. Juanita stops.*)

JUANITA: What's the matter, Parnell? You look sick.

PARNELL: I tried to come sooner. I couldn't get away. Lyle wouldn't let me go.

JUANITA: Were you trying to beat a confession out of him? But you look as though he's been trying to beat a confession out of you. Poor Parnell!

PARNELL: Poor Lyle! He'll never confess. Never. Poor devil!

JUANITA: Poor devil! You weep for Lyle. You're luckier than I am. I can't weep in front of others. I can't say goodbye in front of others. Others don't know what it is you're saying goodbye to.

PARNELL: You loved him.

JUANITA: Yes.

PARNELL: I didn't know.

JUANITA: Ah, you're so lucky, Parnell. I know you didn't know. Tell me, where do you live, Parnell? How can you not know all of the things you do not know?

PARNELL: Why are you hitting out at me? I never thought you cared that much about me. But—oh, Juanita! There are so many things I've never been able to say!

JUANITA: There are so many things you've never been able to hear.

PARNELL: And—you've tried to tell me some of those things?

JUANITA: I used to watch you roaring through this town like a St. George thirsty for dragons. And I wanted to let you know you haven't got to do all that; dragons aren't hard to find, they're everywhere. And nobody wants you to be St. George. We just want you to be Parnell. But, of course, that's much harder.

PARNELL: Are we friends, Juanita? Please say that we're friends.

JUANITA: Friends is not exactly what you mean, Parnell. Tell the truth.

PARNELL: Yes. I've always wanted more than that, from you. But I was afraid you would misunderstand me. That you would feel that I was only trying to exploit you. In another way.

JUANITA: You've been a grown man for a long time now, Parnell. You ought to trust yourself more than that.

PARNELL: I've been a grown man far too long—ever to have dared to dream of offering myself to you.

JUANITA: Your age was never the question, Parnell.

PARNELL: Was there ever any question at all?

JUANITA: Yes. Yes. Yes, once there was.

PARNELL: And there isn't—there can't be—anymore?

JUANITA: No. That train has gone. One day, I'll recover. I'm sure that I'll recover. And I'll see the world again—the marvelous

79

world. And I'll have learned from Richard—how to love. I must. I can't let him die for nothing.

*(Juke box music, loud. The lights change, spot on Parnell's face. Juanita steps across the aisle. Richard appears. They dance. Parnell watches.)*

## Curtain

**END OF ACT TWO**

Two months later. The courtroom.

The courtroom is extremely high, domed, a blinding white emphasized by a dull, somehow ominous gold. The judge's stand is center stage, and at a height. Sloping down from this place on either side, are the black and white townspeople: the jury; photographers and journalists from all over the world; microphones and TV cameras. All windows open: one should be aware of masses of people outside and one should sometimes hear their voices—their roar—as well as singing from the church. The church is directly across the street from the courthouse, and the steeple and the cross are visible throughout the act.

Each witness, when called, is revealed behind scrim and passes through two or three tableaux before moving down the aisle to the witness stand. The witness stand is downstage, in the same place, and at the same angle as the pulpit in Acts I and II.

Before the curtain rises, song: "I Said I Wasn't Going To Tell Nobody, But I Couldn't Keep It To Myself."

The judge's gavel breaks across the singing, and the curtain rises.

# Act III

CLERK (*Calling*): Mrs. Josephine Gladys Britten!

> (*Jo, serving coffee at a church social. She passes out coffee to invisible guests.*)

JO: Am I going to spend the rest of my life serving coffee to strangers in church basements? Am I?—Yes! Reverend Phelps was truly noble! As *usual!*—Reverend Phelps has been married for more than twenty years. Don't let those thoughts into your citadel! You just remember that the mind is a citadel and you can keep out all troubling thoughts!—My! Mrs. Evans! you are certainly a sight for sore eyes! I don't know how you manage to look so unruffled and *cool* and *young!* With all those *children*. And Mr. Evans. How are you tonight?—She has a baby just about every year. I don't know how she stands it. Mr. Evans don't look like that kind of man. You sure can't tell a book by its cover. Lord! I wish I was in my own home and these were *my* guests and my husband was somewhere in the room. I'm getting old! Old! Old maid! *Maid!*—Oh! Mr. Arpino! You taken time out from your engineering to come visit here with us? It sure is a pleasure to have you!—My! He is big! and dark! Like a Greek! or a Spaniard! Some people say he might have a touch of nigger blood. I don't believe that. He's just—*foreign*. That's all. He needs a hair cut. I wonder if he's got hair like that all *over* his body? Remember that your mind is a citadel. A citadel. Oh, Lord, I'm tired of serving coffee in church basements! I want, I want—Why, good evening, Ellis! And Mr. Lyle Britten! We sure don't see either of *you* very often! Why, Mr. Britten! You know you don't mean that! You come over here just to see little old *me?* Why, you just go right ahead and drink that coffee, I do believe you need to be sobered up!

> (*The light changes.*)

REVEREND PHELPS (*Voice*): Do you, Josephine Gladys Miles, take this man, Lyle Britten, Jr., as your lawfully wedded husband, to have and to hold, to love and to cherish, in sickness and in health, till death do you part?

JO: I do. I *do!* Oh, Lyle. I'll make you the best wife any man ever had. I *will.* Love me. Please love me. Look at me! *Look* at me! He *wanted* me. He wanted *me!* I am—Mrs. Josephine Gladys Britten!

(*The light changes again, and Jo takes the stand. We hear the baby crying.*)

BLACKTOWN: Man, that's the southern white lady you supposed to be willing to risk death for!

WHITETOWN: You know, this is a kind of hanging in reverse? Niggers out here to watch us being hanged!

THE STATE: What is your relationship to the accused?

JO: I am his wife.

THE STATE: Will you please tell us, in your own words, of your first meeting with the deceased, Richard Henry?

WHITETOWN: Don't be afraid. Just tell the truth.

BLACKTOWN: Here we go—down the river!

JO: Well, I was in the store, sitting at the counter, and pretty soon this colored boy come in, loud, and talking in just the most awful way. I didn't recognize him, I just knew he wasn't one of *our* colored people. His language was something awful, awful!

THE STATE: He was insulting? Was he insulting, Mrs. Britten?

JO: He said all kinds of things, dirty things, like—well—just like I might have been a colored girl, that's what it sounded like to me. Just like some little colored girl he might have met on a street corner and wanted—wanted to—for a night! And I was scared. I hadn't seen a colored boy act like him before. He acted like he was drunk or crazy or maybe he was under the influence of that dope. I never knew nobody to be *drunk*

83

and act like him. His eyes was just going and he acted like he had a fire in his belly. But I tried to be calm because I didn't want to upset Lyle, you know—Lyle's mighty quick-tempered—and he was working in the back of the store, he was hammering—

THE STATE: Go on, Mrs. Britten. What happened then?

JO: Well, he—that boy—wanted to buy him two Cokes because he had a friend outside—

THE STATE: He brought a friend? He did not come there alone? Did this other boy enter the store?

JO: No, not then he didn't—I—

BLACKTOWN: Come on, bitch. We *know* what you going to say. Get it over with.

JO: I—I give him the two Cokes, and he—tried to grab my hands and pull me to him, and—I—I—he pushed himself up against me, real close and hard—and, oh, he was just like an animal, I could—smell him! And he tried to kiss me, he kept whispering these awful, filthy things and I got scared, I yelled for Lyle! Then Lyle come running out of the back—and when the boy seen I wasn't alone in the store, he yelled for this other boy outside and this other boy come rushing in and they both jumped on Lyle and knocked him down.

THE STATE: What made you decide not to report this incident—this unprovoked assault—to the proper authorities, Mrs. Britten?

JO: We've had so much trouble in this town!

THE STATE: What sort of trouble, Mrs. Britten?

JO: Why, with the colored people! We've got all these northern agitators coming through here all the time, and stirring them up so that you can't hardly sleep nights!

THE STATE: Then you, as a responsible citizen of this town, were doing your best to keep down trouble? Even though you had been so brutally assaulted by a deranged northern Negro dope addict?

JO: Yes. I didn't want to stir up no more trouble. I *made* Lyle keep quiet about it. I thought it would all blow over. I knew the boy's Daddy was a preacher and that he would talk to the boy about the way he was behaving. It was all over town in a second, anyway! And look like all the colored people was on the side of that crazy boy. And Lyle's always been real good to colored people!

(*Laughter from Blacktown.*)

THE STATE: On the evening that the alleged crime was committed— or, rather, the morning—very early on the morning of the 24th of August—where were you and your husband, Mrs. Britten?

JO: We were home. The next day we heard that the boy was missing.

COUNSEL FOR THE BEREAVED: Doesn't an attempt at sexual assault seem a rather strange thing to do, considering that your store is a public place, with people continually going in and out; that, furthermore, it is located on a public road which people use, on foot and in automobiles, all of the time; and considering that your husband, who has the reputation of being a violent man, and who is, in your own words, "mighty quick tempered," was working in the back room?

JO: He didn't know Lyle was back there.

COUNSEL FOR THE BEREAVED: But he knew that someone was back there, for, according to your testimony, "He was hammering."

JO: Well, I told you the boy was crazy. He had to be crazy. Or he was on that dope.

BLACKTOWN: You ever hear of a junkie trying to rape anybody?

JO: *I didn't say rape!*

COUNSEL FOR THE BEREAVED: Were you struggling in Mr. Henry's arms when your husband came out of the back room, carrying his hammer in his hand?

JO: No. I was free then.

COUNSEL FOR THE BEREAVED: Therefore, your husband had only *your* word for the alleged attempted assault! *You* told him that Richard Henry had attempted to assault you? Had made sexual advances to you? Please answer, Mrs. Britten!

JO: Yes. I had—I had to—tell him. I'm his wife!

COUNSEL FOR THE BEREAVED: And a most loyal one. You told your husband that Richard Henry had attempted to assault you and then begged him to do nothing about it?

JO: That's right.

COUNSEL FOR THE BEREAVED: And though he was under the impression that his wife had been nearly raped by a Negro, he agreed to forgive and forget and do nothing about it? He agreed neither to call the law, nor to take the law into his own hands?

JO: Yes.

COUNSEL FOR THE BEREAVED: Extraordinary. Mrs. Britten, you are aware that Richard Henry met his death sometime between the hours of two and five o'clock on the morning of Monday, August 24th?

JO: Yes.

COUNSEL FOR THE BEREAVED: In an earlier statement, several months ago, you stated that your husband had spent that night at the store. You now state that he came in before one o'clock and went to sleep at once. What accounts for this discrepancy?

JO: It's natural. I made a mistake about the time. I got it mixed up with another night. He spent so many nights at that store!

JUDGE: The witness may step down.

(*Jo leaves the stand.*)

CLERK (*Calls*): Mr. Joel Davis!

(*We hear a shot. Papa D. is facing Lyle.*)

LYLE: Why'd you run down there this morning, shooting your mouth off about me and Willa Mae? Why? You been bringing her up here and taking her back all this time, what got into you this morning? Huh? You jealous, old man? Why you come running back here to tell me everything he said? To tell me how he cursed me out? Have you lost your mind? And we been knowing each other all this time. I don't understand you. She ain't the only girl you done brought here for me. Nigger, do you hear me talking to you?

PAPA D.: I didn't think you'd shoot him, Mr. Lyle.

LYLE: I'll shoot any nigger talks to me like that. It was self defense, you hear me? He come in here and tried to kill me. You hear me?

PAPA D.: Yes. Yes sir. I hear you, Mr. Lyle.

LYLE: That's right. You don't say the right thing, nigger, I'll blow your brains out, too.

PAPA D.: Yes sir, Mr. Lyle.

(*Juke box music. Papa D. takes the stand.*)

WHITETOWN: He's worked hard and saved his money and ain't never had no trouble—why can't they all be like that?

BLACKTOWN: Hey, Papa D.! You can't be walking around here without no handkerchief! You might catch cold—after all *these* years!

PAPA D.: Mr. Lyle Britten—he is an *oppressor*. That is the only word for that man. He ain't never give the colored man no kind of chance. I have tried to reason with that man for *years*. I say, Mr. Lyle, look around you. Don't you see that most

87

white folks have changed their way of thinking about us colored folks? I say, Mr. Lyle, we ain't slaves no more and white folks is ready to let us have our chance. Now, why don't you just come on up to where *most* of your people are? and we can make the South a fine place for all of us to live in. That's what I say—and I tried to keep him from being so *hard* on the colored—because I sure do love my people. And I was the closest thing to Mr. Lyle, couldn't nobody else reason with him. But he was *hard*—hard and stubborn. He say, "My folks lived and died this way, and this is the way I'm going to live and die." When he was like that couldn't do nothing with him. I know. I've known him since he was born.

WHITETOWN: He's always been real good to you. You were friends!

BLACKTOWN: You loved him! Tell the truth, mother—tell the truth!

PAPA D.: Yes, we were friends. And, yes, I loved him—in my way. Just like he loved me—in his way.

BLACKTOWN: You knew he was going to kill that boy—didn't you? If you knew it, why didn't you stop him?

PAPA D.: Oh. Ain't none of this easy. What it was, both Mr. Lyle Britten and me, we both love money. And I did a whole lot of things for him, for a long while. Once I had to help him cover up a killing—colored man—I was in too deep myself by that time—you understand? I know you all understand.

BLACKTOWN: Did he kill that boy?

PAPA D.: He come into my joint the night that boy died. The boy was alone, standing at the juke box. We'd been talking— (*Richard, in the juke box light*) If you think you've found all that, Richard—if you think you going to be well now, and you found you somebody who loves you—well, then, I would make tracks out of here. I would—

RICHARD: It's funny, Papa D. I feel like I'm beginning to understand my life—for the first time. I can look back—and it doesn't hurt me like it used to. I want to get Juanita out of here. This is no place for her. They're going to kill her—if she stays here!

PAPA D.: You talk to Juanita about this yet?

RICHARD: No. I haven't talked to nobody about it yet. I just decided it. I guess I'm deciding it now. That's why I'm talking about it now—to you—to see if you'll laugh at me. Do you think she'll laugh at me?

PAPA D.: No. She won't laugh.

RICHARD: I know I can do it. I know I can do it!

PAPA D.: That boy had good sense. He was wild, but he had good sense. And I couldn't blame him too much for being so wild, it seemed to me I knew how he felt.

RICHARD: Papa D., I been in pain and darkness all my life. All my life. And this is the first time in my life I've ever felt—maybe it isn't all like that. Maybe there's more to it than that.

PAPA D.: Lyle Britten come to the door—(*Lyle enters*) He come to the door and he say—

LYLE: You ready for me now, boy? Howdy, Papa D.

PAPA D.: Howdy, Mr. Lyle, how's the world been treating you?

LYLE: I can't complain. You ready, boy?

RICHARD: No. I ain't ready. I got a record to play and a drink to finish.

LYLE: You about ready to close, ain't you, Joel?

PAPA D.: Just about, Mr. Lyle.

RICHARD: I got a record to play. (*Drops coin: juke box music, loud*) And a drink to finish.

89

PAPA D.: He played his record. Lyle Britten never moved from the door. And they just stood there, the two of them, looking at each other. When the record was just about over, the boy come to the bar—he swallowed down the last of his drink.

RICHARD: What do I owe you, Papa D.?

PAPA D.: Oh, you pay me tomorrow. I'm closed now.

RICHARD: What do I owe you, Papa D.? I'm not sure I can pay you tomorrow.

PAPA D.: Give me two dollars.

RICHARD: Here you go. Good night, Papa D. I'm ready, Charlie. (*Exits.*)

PAPA D.: Good night, Richard. Go on home now. Good night, Mr. Lyle. Mr. Lyle!

LYLE: Good night, Joel. You get you some sleep, you hear? (*Exits*)

PAPA D.: Mr. Lyle! Richard! And I never saw that boy again. Lyle killed him. He killed him. I know it, just like I know I'm sitting in this chair. Just like he shot Old Bill and wasn't nothing never, never, never done about it!

JUDGE: The witness may step down.

(*Papa D. leaves the stand.*)

CLERK (*Calls*): Mr. Lorenzo Shannon!

(*We hear a long, loud, animal cry, lonely and terrified: it is Pete, screaming. We discover Lorenzo and Pete, in jail. Night. From far away, we hear Students humming, moaning, singing:* "I Woke Up This Morning With My Mind Stayed On Freedom.")

PETE (*Stammering*): Lorenzo? Lorenzo. I was dreaming—dreaming—dreaming. I was back in that courtyard and Big Jim Byrd's boys was beating us and beating us and beating us—and Big Jim Byrd was laughing. And Anna Mae Taylor was on her knees, she was trying to pray. She say, "Oh, Lord, Lord, Lord, come and help us," and they kept beating on her and beating on her and I saw the blood coming down her neck and they put the prods to her, and, oh, Lorenzo! people was just running around, just crying and moaning and you look to the right and you see somebody go down and you look to the left and you see somebody go down and they was kicking that woman, and I say, "That woman's going to have a baby, don't you kick that woman!" and they say, "No, she ain't going to have no baby," and they knocked me down and they got that prod up between my legs and they say, "You ain't going to be having no babies, neither, nigger!" And then they put that prod to my head—ah! *ah!*—to my *head!* Lorenzo! I can't see right! What have they done to my head? Lorenzo! Lorenzo, am I going to die? Lorenzo—they going to kill us all, ain't they? They mean to kill us all—

LORENZO: Be quiet. Be quiet. They going to come and beat us some more if you don't be quiet.

PETE: Where's Juanita? Did they get Juanita?

LORENZO: I believe Juanita's all right. Go to sleep, Pete. Go to sleep. I won't let you dream. I'll hold you.

(*Lorenzo takes the stand.*)

THE STATE: Did you accompany your late and great friend, Richard Henry, on the morning of August 17, to the store which is owned and run by Mr. and Mrs. Lyle Britten?

LORENZO: We hadn't planned to go there—but we got to walking and talking and we found ourselves there. And it didn't happen like she said. He picked the Cokes out of the box himself, he came to the door with the Cokes in his hand, she hadn't even moved, she was still behind the counter, he never touched that dried out little peckerwood!

WHITETOWN: Get that nigger! Who does that nigger think he is!

91

BLACKTOWN: Speak, Lorenzo! Go, my man!

THE STATE: You cannot expect this courtroom to believe that so serious a battle was precipitated by the question of twenty cents! There was some other reason. What was this reason? Had he—and you—been drinking?

LORENZO: It was early in the day, Cap'n. We ain't rich enough to drink in the daytime.

THE STATE: Or *smoking*, perhaps? Perhaps your friend had just had his quota of heroin for the day, and was feeling jolly— in a mood to *prove* to you what he had already suggested with those filthy photographs of himself and naked white women!

LORENZO: I never saw no photographs. White women are a problem for white men. We had not been drinking. All we was smoking was that same goddamn tobacco that made *you* rich because we picked it for you for nothing, and carried it to market for you for nothing. And I *know* ain't no heroin in this town because none of you mothers need it. You was *born* frozen. Richard was better than that. I'd rather die than be like you, Cap'n, but I'd be *proud* to be like Richard. That's all I can tell you, Mr. Boss-Man. But I know he wasn't trying to rape nobody. Rape!

THE STATE: Your Honor, will you instruct the witness that he is under oath, that this is a court of law, and that it is a serious matter to be held in contempt of court!

LORENZO: More serious than the chain gang? *I* know I'm under oath. If there was any reason, it was just that Richard couldn't stand white people. *Couldn't stand white people!* And, now, do you want me to tell you all that I know about *that*? Do you think you could stand it? You'd cut my tongue out before you'd let me tell you all that I know about *that*!

COUNSEL FOR THE BEREAVED: You are a student here?

LORENZO: In my spare time. I just come off the chain gang a couple of days ago. I was trespassing in the white waiting room of the bus station.

COUNSEL FOR THE BEREAVED: What are you studying—in your spare time—Mr. Shannon?

LORENZO: History.

COUNSEL FOR THE BEREAVED: To your knowledge—during his stay in this town—was the late Mr. Richard Henry still addicted to narcotics?

LORENZO: No. He'd kicked his habit. He'd paid his dues. He was just trying to live. And he almost made it.

COUNSEL FOR THE BEREAVED: You were very close to him?

LORENZO: Yes.

COUNSEL FOR THE BEREAVED: To your knowledge—was he carrying about obscene photographs of himself and naked white women?

LORENZO: To my knowledge—and I would know—no. The only times he ever opened a popular magazine was to look at the Jazz Poll. No. They been asking me about photographs they say he was carrying and they been asking me about a gun I never saw. No. It wasn't like that. He was a beautiful cat, and they killed him. That's all. That's *all*.

JUDGE: The witness may step down.

LORENZO: Well! I thank you kindly. *Suh!*

(*Lorenzo leaves the stand.*)

CLERK (*Calls*): Miss Juanita Harmon!

(*Juanita rises from bed; early Sunday morning.*)

JUANITA: He lay beside me on that bed like a rock. As heavy as a rock—like he'd fallen—fallen from a high place—fallen so far and landed so heavy, he seemed almost to be sinking out of sight—with one knee pointing to heaven. My God. He covered me like that. He wasn't at all like I thought he was. He fell on—fell on me—like life and death. My God. His chest, his belly, the rising and the falling, the moans. How he clung, how he struggled—life and death! Life and death! Why did it all seem to me like tears? That he came to me, clung to me, plunged into me, sobbing, howling, bleeding, somewhere inside his chest, his belly, and it all came out, came pouring out, like tears! My God, the smell, the touch, the taste, the sound, of anguish! Richard! Why couldn't I have held you closer? Held you, held you, borne you, given you life again! Have made you be born again! Oh, Richard. The teeth that gleamed, oh! when you smiled, the spit flying when you cursed, the teeth stinging when you bit—your breath, your hands, your weight, my God, when you moved in me! Where shall I go now, what shall I do? Oh. Oh. Oh. Mama was frightened. Frightened because little Juanita brought her first real lover to this house. I suppose God does for Mama what Richard did for me. Juanita! I don't care! I don't care! Yes, I want a lover made of flesh and blood, of flesh and blood, like me, I don't want to be God's mother! He can *have* His icy, snow-white heaven! If He is somewhere around this fearful planet, if I ever see Him, I will spit in His face! In God's face! How *dare* He presume to judge a living soul! A living soul. Mama is afraid I'm pregnant. Mama is afraid of so much. I'm not afraid. I hope I'm pregnant. I *hope* I am! One more illegitimate black baby— that's right, you jive mothers! And I am going to raise my baby to be a man. A *man*, you dig? Oh, let me be pregnant, let me be pregnant, don't let it all be gone! A man. Juanita. A man. Oh, my God, there are no more. For me. Did this happen to Mama sometime? Did she have a man sometime who vanished like smoke? And left her to get through this world as best she could? Is that why she married my father?

Did this happen to Mother Henry? Is this how we all get to be mothers—so soon? of helpless men—because all the other men perish? No. No. No. No. What is this world like? I will end up taking care of some man, some day. Help me do it with love. Pete. Meridian. Parnell. We have been the mothers for them all. It must be dreadful to be Parnell. There is no flesh he can touch. All of it is bloody. Incest everywhere. Ha-ha! You're going crazy, Juanita. Oh, Lord, don't let me go mad. Let me be pregnant! Let me be pregnant!

(*Juanita takes the stand. One arm is in a sling.*)

BLACKTOWN: Look! You should have seen her when she *first* come out of jail! Why we always got to love *them?* How come it's *us* always got to do the loving? Because you *black*, mother! Everybody knows we *strong* on loving! Except when it comes to our women.

WHITETOWN: Black slut! What happened to her arm? Somebody had to twist it, I reckon. She looks like she might be a right pretty little girl—why is she messing up her life this way?

THE STATE: Miss Harmon, you have testified that you were friendly with the mother of the deceased. How old were you when she died?

JUANITA: I was sixteen.

THE STATE: Sixteen! You are older than the deceased?

JUANITA: By two years.

THE STATE: At the time of his mother's death, were you and Richard Henry considering marriage?

JUANITA: No. Of course not.

THE STATE: The question of marriage did not come up until just before he died?

JUANITA: Yes.

95

THE STATE: But between the time that Richard Henry left this town and returned, you had naturally attracted other boy friends?

BLACKTOWN: Why don't you come right out and ask her if she's a virgin, man? Save you time.

WHITETOWN: She probably pregnant right now—and don't know who the father is. That's the way they are.

THE STATE: The departure of the boy and the death of the mother must have left all of you extremely lonely?

JUANITA: It can't be said to have made us any happier.

THE STATE: Reverend Henry missed his wife, you missed your play-mate. His grief and your common concern for the boy must have drawn you closer together?

BLACKTOWN: Oh, man! Get to *that!*

WHITETOWN: That's right. What about that liver-lipped preacher?

THE STATE: Miss Harmon, you describe yourself as a student. Where have you spent the last few weeks?

JUANITA: In jail! I was arrested for—

THE STATE: I am not concerned with the reasons for your arrest. How much time, all told, have you spent in jail?

JUANITA: It would be hard to say—a long time.

THE STATE: Excellent preparation for your future! Is it not true, Miss Harmon, that before the late Richard Henry returned to this town, you were considering marriage with another so-called student, Pete Spivey? Can you seriously expect this court to believe anything you now say concerning Richard Henry? Would you not say the same thing, and for the same reason, concerning the father? Concerning Pete Spivey? And how many others!

WHITETOWN: That's the way they are. It's not their fault. That's what they want us to integrate with.

BLACKTOWN: These people are sick. Sick. Sick people's been known to be made well by a little shedding of blood.

JUANITA: I am not responsible for your imagination.

THE STATE: What do you know of the fight which took place between Richard Henry and Lyle Britten, at Mr. Britten's store?

JUANITA: I was not a witness to that fight.

THE STATE: But you had seen Richard Henry before the fight? Was he sober?

JUANITA: Yes.

THE STATE: You can swear to that?

JUANITA: Yes, I can swear to it.

THE STATE: And you saw him after the fight? Was he sober then?

JUANITA: Yes. He was sober then. (*Courtroom in silhouette*) I heard about the fight at the end of the day—when I got home. And I went running to Reverend Henry's house. And I met him on the porch—just sitting there.

THE STATE: You met whom?

JUANITA: I met—Richard.

(*We discover Meridian.*)

MERIDIAN: Hello, Juanita. Don't look like that.

JUANITA: Meridian, what happened today? Where's Richard?

MERIDIAN: He's all right now. He's sleeping. We better send him away. Lyle's dangerous. You know that. (*Takes Juanita in his arms; then holds her at arm's length*) You'll go with him. Won't you?

JUANITA: Meridian—oh, my God.

MERIDIAN: Juanita, tell me something I have to know. I'll never ask it again.

JUANITA: Yes, Meridian—

MERIDIAN: Before he came—I wasn't just making it all up, was I? There was something at least—beginning—something dimly possible—wasn't there? I thought about you so much—and it was so wonderful each time I saw you—and I started hoping as I haven't let myself hope, oh, for a long time. I knew you were much younger, and I'd known you since you were a child. But I thought that maybe that didn't matter, after all—we got on so well together. I wasn't making it all up, was I?

JUANITA: No. You weren't making it up—not all of it, anyway, there was something there. We were lonely. You were hoping. I was hoping, too—oh, Meridian! Of all the people on God's earth I would rather die than hurt!

MERIDIAN: Hush, Juanita. I know that. I just wanted to be told that I hadn't lost my mind. I've lost so much. I think there's something wrong in being—what I've become—something really wrong. I mean, I think there's something wrong with allowing oneself to become so lonely. I think that I was proud that I could bear it. Each day became a kind of test—to see if I could bear it. And there were many days when I couldn't bear it—when I walked up and down and howled and lusted and cursed and prayed—just like any man. And I've been—I haven't been as celibate as I've seemed. But my confidence—my confidence—was destroyed back there when I pulled back that rug they had her covered with and I saw that little face on that broken neck. There wasn't any blood—just water. She was soaked. Oh, my God. My God. And I haven't trusted myself with a woman since. I keep seeing her the last time I saw her, whether I'm awake or asleep. That's why I let you get away from me. It wasn't my son that did it. It was me. And so much the better for you. And him. And I've held it all in since then—what fearful choices we must make! In order not to commit murder, in order not to

98

become too monstrous, in order to be some kind of example to my only son. Come. Let me be an example now. And kiss you on the forehead and wish you well.

JUANITA: Meridian. Meridian. Will it always be like this? Will life always be like this? Must we always suffer so?

MERIDIAN: I don't know, Juanita. I know that we must bear what we must bear. Don't cry, Juanita. Don't cry. Let's go on on.

*(Exits.)*

JUANITA: By and by Richard woke up and I was there. And we tried to make plans to go, but he said he wasn't going to run no more from white folks—never no more!—but was going to stay and be a man—a *man!*—right here. And I couldn't *make* him see differently. I knew what he meant, I knew how he felt, but I didn't want him to die! And by the time I persuaded him to take *me* away, to take *me* away from this terrible place, it was too late. Lyle killed him. Lyle killed him! Like they been killing all our men, for years, for generations! Our husbands, our fathers, our brothers, our sons!

JUDGE: The witness may step down.

*(Juanita leaves the stand. Mother Henry helps her to her seat.)*

This court is adjourned until ten o'clock tomorrow morning.

*(Chaos and cacophony. The courtroom begins to empty. Reporters rush to phone booths and to witnesses. Light bulbs flash. We hear snatches of the Journalists' reports, in their various languages. Singing from the church. Blackout. The next and last day of the trial. Even more crowded and tense.)*

CLERK *(Calls)*: Mrs. Wilhelmina Henry!

*(Mother Henry, in street clothes, walks down the aisle, takes the stand.)*

THE STATE: You are Mrs. Wilhelmina Henry?

MOTHER HENRY: Yes.

99

THE STATE: Mrs. Henry, you—and your husband, until he died—lived in this town all your lives and never had any trouble. We've always gotten on well down here.

MOTHER HENRY: No white man never called my husband Mister, neither, not as long as he lived. Ain't no white man never called *me* Mrs. Henry before today. I had to get a grandson killed for that.

THE STATE: Mrs. Henry, your grief elicits my entire sympathy, and the sympathy of every white man in this town. But is it not true, Mrs. Henry, that your grandson arrived in this town armed? He was carrying a gun and, apparently, had carried a gun for years.

MOTHER HENRY: I don't know where you got that story, or why you keep harping on it. *I* never saw no gun.

THE STATE: You are under oath, Mrs. Henry.

MOTHER HENRY: I don't need you to tell me I'm under oath. I been under oath all my life. And I tell you, I never saw no gun.

THE STATE: Mrs. Henry, did you ever see your grandson behaving strangely—as though he were under the influence of strong drugs?

MOTHER HENRY: No. Not since he was six and they pulled out his tonsils. They gave him ether. *He* didn't act as strange as his Mama and Daddy. He just went on to sleep. But they like to had a fit. (*Richard's song*) I remember the day he was born. His mother had a hard time holding him and a hard time getting him here. But here he come, in the wintertime, late and big and loud. And my boy looked down into his little son's face and he said, "God give us a son. God's give us a son. Lord, help us to raise him to be a good strong man."

JUDGE: The witness may step down.

CLERK (*Calls*): Reverend Meridian Henry!

(*Blackout. Meridian, in Sunday School. The class itself, predominately adolescent girls, is in silhouette.*)

MERIDIAN: —And here is the prophet, Solomon, the son of David, looking down through the ages, and speaking of Christ's love for His church. *(Reads)* How fair is thy love, my sister, my spouse! How much better is thy love than wine! and the smell of thine ointments than all spices! *(Pause. The silhouette of girls vanishes)* Oh, that it were one man, speaking to one woman!

*(Blackout. Meridian takes the stand.)*

BLACKTOWN: I wonder how he feels now about all that turn-the-other-cheek jazz. His son sure didn't go for it.

WHITETOWN: That's the father. Claims to be a preacher. He brought this on himself. He's been raising trouble in this town for a long time.

THE STATE: You are Reverend Meridian Henry?

MERIDIAN: That is correct.

THE STATE: And you are the father of the late Richard Henry?

MERIDIAN: Yes.

THE STATE: You are a minister?

MERIDIAN: A Christian minister—yes.

THE STATE: And you raised your son according to the precepts of the Christian church?

MERIDIAN: I tried. But both my son and I had profound reservations concerning the behavior of Christians. He wondered why they treated black people as they do. And I was unable to give him—a satisfactory answer.

THE STATE: But certainly you—as a Christian minister—did not encourage your son to go armed?

MERIDIAN: The question never came up. He was not armed.

THE STATE: He was not armed?

MERIDIAN: No.

THE STATE: You never saw him with a gun? Or with any other weapon?

MERIDIAN: No.

THE STATE: Reverend Henry—are you in a position to swear that your son never carried arms?

MERIDIAN: Yes. I can swear to it. The only time the subject was ever mentioned he told me that he was stronger than white people and he could live without a gun.

BLACKTOWN: I bet he didn't say how.

WHITETOWN: That liver-lipped nigger is lying. He's lying!

THE STATE: Perhaps the difficulties your son had in accepting the Christian faith is due to your use of the pulpit as a forum for irresponsible notions concerning social equality, Reverend Henry. Perhaps the failure of the son is due to the failure of the father.

MERIDIAN: I am afraid that the gentleman flatters himself. I do not wish to see Negroes become the equal of their murderers. I wish us to become equal to ourselves. To become a people so free in themselves that they will have no need to—fear—others—and have no need to murder others.

THE STATE: You are not in the pulpit now. I am suggesting that you are responsible—directly responsible!--for your son's tragic fate.

MERIDIAN: I know more about that than you do. But you cannot consider my son's death to have been tragic. For you, it would have been tragic if he had lived.

THE STATE: With such a father, it is remarkable that the son lived as long as he did.

MERIDIAN: Remarkable, too, that the father lived!

THE STATE: Reverend Henry—you have been a widower for how many years?

MERIDIAN: I have been a widower for nearly eight years.

THE STATE: You are a young man still?

MERIDIAN: Are you asking me my age? I am not young.

THE STATE: You are not old. It must have demanded great discipline—

MERIDIAN: To live among you? Yes.

THE STATE: What is your relationship to the young, so-called student, Miss Juanita Harmon?

MERIDIAN: I am her old friend. I had hoped to become her father-in-law.

THE STATE: You are nothing more than old friends?

WHITETOWN: That's right. Get it out of him. Get the truth out of him.

BLACKTOWN: Leave the man *something*. Leave him something!

THE STATE: You have been celibate since the death of your wife?

BLACKTOWN: He never said he was a monk, you jive mother!

WHITETOWN: Make him tell us all about it. *All* about it.

MERIDIAN: Celibate? How does my celibacy concern you?

THE STATE: Your Honor, will you instruct the witness that he is on the witness stand, not I, and that he must answer the questions put to him!

MERIDIAN: *The questions put to him!* All right. Do you accept this answer? I am a man. A *man!* I tried to help my son become a man. But manhood is a dangerous pursuit, here. And that pursuit undid him because of *your* guns, *your* hoses, *your* dogs, *your* judges, *your* law-makers, *your* folly, *your* pride, *your* cruelty, *your* cowardice, *your* money, *your* chain gangs, and *your* churches! Did you think it would endure forever? that we would pay for *your* ease forever?

BLACKTOWN: Speak, my man! Amen! Amen! Amen! Amen!

WHITETOWN: Stirring up hate! Stirring up hate! A *preacher*—stirring up hate!

MERIDIAN: Yes! I *am* responsible for the death of my son. I—hoped—I prayed—I struggled—so that the world would be different by the time he was a man than it had been when he was born. And I thought that—then—when he looked at me—he would think that I—his father—had helped to change it.

THE STATE: What about those photographs your son carried about with him? Those photographs of himself and naked white women?

BLACKTOWN: Man! Would I love to look in *your* wallet!

WHITETOWN: Make him tell us about it, make him tell us *all* about it!

MERIDIAN: Photographs? My son and naked white women? He never mentioned them to me.

THE STATE: You were closer than most fathers and sons?

MERIDIAN: I never took a poll on most fathers and sons.

THE STATE: You never discussed women?

MERIDIAN: We talked about his mother. She was a woman. We talked about Miss Harmon. *She* is a woman. But we never talked about dirty pictures. We didn't need that.

THE STATE: Reverend Henry, you have made us all aware that your love for your son transcends your respect for the truth or your devotion to the church. But—luckily for the truth—it is a matter of public record that your son was so dangerously deranged that it was found necessary, for his own sake, to incarcerate him. It was at the end of that incarceration that he returned to this town. We know that his life in the North was riotous—he brought that riot into this town. The evidence is overwhelming. And yet, you, a Christian minister, dare to bring us this tissue of lies in defense of a known pimp, dope addict, and rapist! You are yourself so eaten up by race hatred that no word of yours can be believed.

MERIDIAN: Your judgment of myself and my motives cannot concern me at all. I have lived with that judgment far too long. The truth cannot be heard in this dreadful place. But I will tell you again what I know. I know why my son became a dope addict. I know better than you will ever know, even if I should explain it to you for all eternity, how I am responsible for that. But I know my son was not a pimp. He respected women far too much for that. And I know he was not a rapist. Rape is hard work—and, frankly, I don't think that the alleged object was my son's type at all!

THE STATE: And you are a minister?

MERIDIAN: I think I may be beginning to become one.

JUDGE: The witness may step down.

(*Meridian leaves the stand.*)

CLERK (*Calls*): Mr. Parnell James!

(*Parnell in his bedroom, dressed in a bathrobe. Night.*)

PARNELL: She says I called somebody else's name. What name could I have called? And she won't repeat the name. Well. That's enough to freeze the blood and arrest the holy, the liberating orgasm! Christ, how weary I am of this dull calisthenic called love—with no love in it! What name could I have called? I hope it was—a *white* girl's name, anyway! Ha-ha! How still she became! And I hardly realized it, I was too far away—and then it was too late. And she was just looking at me. Jesus! To have somebody just looking at you—just looking at you—like that—at such a moment! It makes you feel—like you woke up and found yourself in bed with your mother! I tried to find out what was wrong—poor girl! But there's nothing you can say at a moment like that—really nothing. You're caught. Well, haven't I kept telling

105

her that there's no future for her with me? There's no future for me with anybody! But that's all right. What name could I have called? I haven't been with anybody else for a long time, a long time. She says I haven't been with her, either. I guess she's right. I've just been using her. Using her as an anchor—to hold me here, in this house, this bed—so I won't find myself on the other side of town, ruining my reputation. *What* reputation? They all know. I swear they all *know*. Know what? What's there to know? So you get drunk and you fool around a little. Come on, Parnell. There's more to it than that. That's the reason you draw blanks whenever you get drunk. Everything comes out. Everything. They see what you don't dare to see. What name could I have called? Richard would say that you've got—black fever! Yeah, and he'd be wrong—that long, loud, black mother. I wonder if she's asleep yet—or just lying there, looking at the walls. Poor girl! All your life you've been made sick, stunned, dizzy, oh, Lord! driven half mad by blackness. Blackness in front of your eyes. Boys and girls, men and women—you've bowed down in front of them all! And then hated yourself. Hated yourself for debasing yourself? Out with it, Parnell! The nigger-lover! Black boys and girls! I've wanted my hands full of them, wanted to drown them, laughing and dancing and making love—making love—wow!—and be transformed, formed, liberated out of this grey-white envelope. Jesus! I've always been afraid. Afraid of what I saw in their eyes? They don't love me, certainly. You don't love them, either! Sick with a disease only white men catch. Blackness. What is it like to be black? To look out on the world from *that* place? I give nothing! How dare she say that! My girl, if you knew what I've given! Ah. Come off it, Parnell. To *whom* have you given? What name did I call? What name did I call?

(*Blackout. Parnell and Lyle. Hunting on Parnell's land.*)

LYLE: You think it's a good idea, then? You think she won't say no?

PARNELL: Well, you're the one who's got to go through it. *You've* got to ask for Miss Josephine's hand in marriage. And then you've got to live with her—for the rest of your life. Watch that gun. I've never seen you so jumpy. I might say it was a good idea if I thought she'd say no. But I think she'll say yes.

LYLE: Why would she say yes to me?

PARNELL: I think she's drawn to you. It isn't hard to be—drawn to you. Don't you know that?

LYLE: No. When I was young, I used to come here sometimes—with my Daddy. He didn't like *your* Daddy a-*tall!* We used to steal your game, Parnell—you didn't know that, did you?

PARNELL: I think I knew it.

LYLE: We shot at the game and your Daddy's overseers shot at us. But we *got* what *we* came after. *They* never got *us!*

PARNELL: You're talking an awful lot today. You nervous about Miss Josephine?

LYLE: Wait a minute. You think I ought to marry Jo?

PARNELL: I don't know who anybody should marry. Do you want to marry Jo?

LYLE: Well—I got to marry somebody. I got to have some kids. And Jo is—*clean!*

(*Parnell sights, shoots.*)

PARNELL: Goddamn!

LYLE: Missed it. Ha-ha!

PARNELL: It's probably somebody's mother.

LYLE: Watch. (*Sights, shoots*) Ha-ha!

PARNELL: Bravo!

LYLE: I knew it! Had my name written on it, just as pretty as you please! (*Exits, returns with his bird*) See? My Daddy taught me well. It was sport for you. It was life for us.

PARNELL: I reckon you shot somebody's baby.

LYLE: I tell you—I can't go on like this. There comes a time in a man's life when he's got to have him a little—peace.

PARNELL: You mean calm. Tranquillity.

LYLE: Yeah. I didn't mean it like it sounded. You thought I meant— no. I'm tired of—

PARNELL: Poon-tang.

LYLE: How'd you know? You tired of it, too? Hell. Yeah. I want kids.

PARNELL: Well, then—marry the girl.

LYLE: She ain't a girl no more. It might be her last chance, too. But, I swear, Parnell, she might be the only virgin left in this town. The only *white* virgin. I can vouch for the fact ain't many black ones.

PARNELL: You've been active, I know. Any kids?

LYLE: None that I know of. Ha-ha!

PARNELL: Do you think Jo might be upset—by the talk about you and Old Bill? She's real respectable, you know. She's a *librarian.*

LYLE: No. Them things happen every day. You think I ought to marry her? You really think she'll say yes?

PARNELL: She'll say yes. She'd better. I wish you luck. Name the first one after me.

LYLE: No. You be the godfather. And my best man. I'm going to name the first one after my Daddy—because he taught me more about hunting on your land than *you* know. I'll give him your middle name. I'll call him Lyle Parnell Britten, Jr.!

PARNELL: If the girl says yes.

LYLE: Well, if she says no, ain't no problem, is there? We know where to go when the going gets rough, don't we, old buddy?

PARNELL: Do we? Look! Mine?

LYLE: What'll you bet?

PARNELL: The price of your wedding rings.

LYLE: You're on. Mine? *Mine!*

(*Blackout. Parnell walks down the aisle, takes the stand.*)

WHITETOWN:

Here comes the nigger-lover!
But I bet you one thing—he knows more about the truth in this case than anybody else.
He ought to—he's with them all the time.
It's sad when a man turns against his own people!

BLACKTOWN:

Let's see how the Negro's friend comes through!
They been waiting for *him*—they going to tear his behind *up!*
I don't trust him. I *never* trusted him!
*Why?* Because he's *white*, that's why!

THE STATE: You were acquainted with the late Richard Henry?

PARNELL: Of course. His father and I have been friends all our lives.

THE STATE: Close friends?

PARNELL: Yes. Very close.

THE STATE: And what is your relationship to the alleged murderer, Mr. Lyle Britten?

PARNELL: We, also, have been friends all our lives.

THE STATE: Close friends?

PARNELL: Yes.

THE STATE: As close as the friendship between yourself and the dead boy's father?

PARNELL: I would say so—it was a very different relationship.

THE STATE: Different in what respect, Mr. James?

PARNELL: Well, we had different things to talk about. We did different things together.

THE STATE: What sort of different things?

PARNELL: Well—hunting, for example—things like that.

THE STATE: You never went hunting with Reverend Henry?

PARNELL: No. He didn't like to hunt.

THE STATE: He told you so? He told you that he didn't like to hunt?

PARNELL: The question never came up. We led very different lives.

THE STATE: I am gratified to hear it. Is it not true, Mr. James, that it is impossible for any two people to go on a hunting trip together if either of them has any reason at all to distrust the other?

PARNELL: Well, of course that would have to be true. But it's never talked about—it's just understood.

THE STATE: We can conclude, then, that you were willing to trust Lyle Britten with your life but did not feel the same trust in Reverend Henry?

PARNELL: Sir, you may not draw any such conclusion! I have told you that Reverend Henry and I led very different lives!

THE STATE: But you have been friends all your lives. Reverend Henry is also a southern boy—he, also, I am sure, knows and loves this land, has gone swimming and fishing in her streams and rivers, and stalked game in her forests. And yet, close as you are, you have never allowed yourself to be alone with Reverend Henry when Reverend Henry had a gun. Doesn't this suggest some *lack*—in your vaunted friendship?

PARNELL: Your suggestion is unwarranted and unworthy. As a soldier, I have often been alone with Negroes with guns, and it certainly never caused me any uneasiness.

THE STATE: But you were fighting a common enemy then. What was your impression of the late Richard Henry?

PARNELL: I liked him. He was very outspoken and perhaps tactless, but a very valuable person.

THE STATE: How would you describe his effect on this town? Among his own people? Among the whites?

PARNELL: His effect? He was pretty well liked.

THE STATE: That does not answer my question.

PARNELL: His effect was—kind of unsettling, I suppose. After all, he had lived in the North a long time, he wasn't used to—the way we do things down here.

THE STATE: He was accustomed to the way things are done in the North—where he learned to carry arms, to take dope, and to couple with white women!

PARNELL: I cannot testify to any of that, sir. I can only repeat that he reacted with great intensity to the racial situation in this town, and his effect on the town was, to that extent, unsettling.

THE STATE: Did he not encourage the Negroes of this town to arm?

PARNELL: Not to my knowledge, sir, no. And, in any case, they are not armed.

THE STATE: You are in a position to reassure us on this point?

PARNELL: My friends do not lie.

THE STATE: You are remarkably fortunate. You are aware of the attitude of the late Richard Henry toward white women? You saw the photographs he carried about with him?

PARNELL: We never discussed women. I never saw the photographs.

THE STATE: But you knew of their existence?

PARNELL: They were not obscene. They were simply snapshots of people he had known in the North.

THE STATE: Snapshots of white women?

PARNELL: Yes.

THE STATE: You are the first witness to admit the existence of these photographs, Mr. James.

PARNELL: It is very likely that the other witnesses never saw them. The boy had been discouraged, very early on, from mentioning them or showing them about.

THE STATE: Discouraged by whom?

PARNELL: Why—by—me.

THE STATE: But you never saw the photographs—

PARNELL: I told him I didn't want to see them and that it would be dangerous to carry them about.

THE STATE: He showed these photographs to you, but to no one else?

PARNELL: That would seem to be the case, yes.

THE STATE: What was his motive in taking you into his confidence?

PARNELL: Bravado. He wanted me to know that he had white friends in the North, that—he had been happy—in the North.

THE STATE: You did not tell his father? You did not warn your close friend?

PARNELL: I am sure that Richard never mentioned these photographs to his father. He would have been too ashamed. Those women were beneath him.

THE STATE: A white woman who surrenders to a colored man is beneath all human consideration. She has wantonly and deliberately defiled the temple of the Holy Ghost. It is clear to me that the effect of such a boy on this town was irresponsible and incendiary to the greatest degree. Did you not find your close friendship with Reverend Henry somewhat strained by the son's attempt to rape the wife of your other close friend, Lyle Britten?

PARNELL: This attempt was never mentioned before—before today.

THE STATE: You are as close as you claim to the Britten family and knew nothing of this attempted rape? How do you explain that?

PARNELL: I cannot explain it.

THE STATE: This is a court of law, Mr. James, and we will have the truth!

WHITETOWN: Make him tell the truth!

BLACKTOWN: Make him tell the truth!

THE STATE: How can you be the close friend you claim to be of the Britten family and not have known of so grave an event?

PARNELL: I—I knew of a fight. It was understood that the boy had gone to Mr. Britten's store looking for a fight. I—I cannot explain *that*, either.

THE STATE: Who told you of the fight?

PARNELL: Why—Mr. Britten.

THE STATE: And did not tell you that Richard Henry had attempted to assault his wife? Come, Mr. James!

PARNELL: We were all very much upset. Perhaps he was not as coherent as he might have been—perhaps I failed to listen closely. It was my assumption that Mrs. Britten had misconstrued the boy's actions—he had been in the North a long time, his manner was very free and bold.

THE STATE: Mrs. Britten has testified that Richard Henry grabbed her and pulled her to him and tried to kiss her. How can those actions be misconstrued?

PARNELL: Those actions are—quite explicit.

THE STATE: Thank you, Mr. James. That is all.

JUDGE: The witness may step down.

(*Parnell leaves the stand.*)

BLACKTOWN: What do you think of our fine friend *now?* He didn't do it to us rough and hard. No, he was real gentle. I hardly felt a thing. Did you? You can't never go against the word of a white lady, man, not even if you're white. Can't be done. He was sad. *Sad!*

WHITETOWN: It took him long enough! He did his best not to say it—can you imagine! So her story was true—after all! I hope he's learned his lesson. We been trying to tell him—for years!

CLERK (*Calls*): Mr. Lyle Britten!

(*Lyle, in the woods*)

LYLE: I wonder what he'll grow up to look like. Of course, it might be a girl. I reckon I wouldn't mind—just keep on trying till I get me a boy, ha-ha! Old Miss Josephine is something, ain't she? I really struck oil when I come across her. She's a nice woman. And she's *my* woman—I ain't got to worry about *that* a-tall! You're making big changes in your life, Lyle, and you got to be ready to take on this extra responsibility. Shoot, I'm ready. I know what I'm doing. And I'm going to work harder than I've ever worked before in my life to make Jo happy—and keep her happy—and raise our children to be fine men and women. Lord, you know I'm not a praying man. I've done a lot of wrong things in my life and I ain't never going to be perfect. I know You know that. I know You understand that. But, Lord, hear me today and help me to do what I'm supposed to do. I want to be as strong as my Mama and Daddy and raise my children like they raised me. That's what I want, oh Lord. In a few years I'll be walking here, showing my son these trees and this water and this sky. He'll have his hand in my hand, and I'll show him the world. Isn't that a funny thing! He don't even exist yet—he's just an egg in his mother's belly, I bet you couldn't even find him with a microscope—and I put him there—and he's coming out soon—with fingers and toes and eyes—and by and by, he'll learn to walk and talk—and I reckon I'll have to spank him sometime—if he's anything like me, I know I will. Isn't that something! My son! Hurry up and get here, so I can hug you in my arms and give you a good start on your long journey!

(*Blackout. Lyle, with Papa D. Drunk. Music and dancing*)

LYLE: You remember them days when Willa Mae was around? My mind's been going back to them days. You remember? She was a hot little piece, I just had to have some of that, I just *had* to. Half the time she didn't wear no stockings, just had them brown, round legs just moving. I couldn't keep my eyes off her legs when she didn't wear no stockings. And you know what she told me? You know what she told me? She said there wasn't a nigger alive could be as good to her as me. That's right. She said she'd like to *see* the nigger could do her like I done her. You hear me, boy? That's something, ain't it? Boy—she'd just come into a room sometimes and my old pecker would stand up at attention. You ain't jealous, are you, Joel? Ha-ha! You never did hear from her no more, did you? No, I reckon you didn't. Shoot, I got to get on home. I'm a family man now, I got—great responsibilities! Yeah. Be seeing you, Joel. You don't want to close up and walk a-ways with me, do you? No, I reckon you better not. They having fun. Sure wish I could be more like you all. Bye-bye!

(*Blackout. As Lyle approaches the witness stand, the lights in the courtroom dim. We hear voices from the church, singing a lament. The lights come up.*)

JUDGE: Gentlemen of the jury, have you reached a verdict?

FOREMAN: We have, Your Honor.

JUDGE: Will the prisoner please rise?
*(Lyle rises.)*
Do you find the defendant, Mr. Lyle Britten, guilty or not guilty?

FOREMAN: Not guilty, Your Honor.
*(Cheering in* WHITETOWN. *Silence in* BLACKTOWN. *The stage is taken over by Reporters, Photographers, Witnesses, Townspeople. Lyle is congratulated and embraced.* BLACK-TOWN *files out silently, not looking back.* WHITETOWN *files out jubilantly, and yet with a certain reluctance. Presently, the stage is empty, except for Lyle, Jo, Mother Henry, Meridian, Parnell, Juanita, and Lorenzo.)*

JO: Let's get out of here and go home. We've been here just for days. I wouldn't care if I *never* saw the insides of a court-room again! Let's go home, sugar. We got something to celebrate!

JUANITA: We, too, must go—to another celebration. We're having a prayer meeting on the City Hall steps.

LORENZO: Prayer meeting!

LYLE: Well, it was touch and go there for awhile, Parnell, but you sure come through. I knew you would.

JO: Let's go, Lyle. The baby's hungry.

MERIDIAN: Perhaps now you can ask him to tell you the truth. He's got nothing to lose now. They can't try him again.

LYLE: Wasn't much sense in trying me now, this time, was there, Reverend? These people have been knowing me and my good Jo here all our lives, they ain't going to doubt us. And you people—you people—ought to have better sense and more things to do than running around stirring up all this hate and trouble. *That's* how your son got himself killed. He listened to crazy niggers like you!

MERIDIAN: Did you kill him?

LYLE: They just asked me that in court, didn't they? And they just decided I didn't, didn't they? Well, that's good enough for me and all those white people and so it damn sure better be good enough for you!

PARNELL: That's no answer. It's not good enough for me.

LYLE: What do you mean, that's no answer? Why isn't it an answer? Why isn't it good enough for you? You know, when you were up on the stand right now, you acted like you doubted my Jo's word. You got no right to doubt Jo's word. You ain't no better than she is! You ain't no better than me!

PARNELL: I am aware of that. God knows I have been made aware of that—for the first time in my life. But, as you and I will never be the same again—since our comedy is finished, since I have failed you so badly—let me say this. I did not doubt Jo's word. I knew that she was lying and that you had made her lie. That was a terrible thing to do to her. It was a terrible thing that I just did to you. I really don't know if what I did to Meridian was as awful as what I did to you. I don't expect forgiveness, Meridian. I only hope that all of us will suffer past this agony and horror.

LYLE: What's the matter with you? Have you forgotten you a white man? A white man! My Daddy told me not to *never* forget I was a white man! Here I been knowing you all my life—and now I'm ashamed of you. Ashamed of you! Get on over to niggertown! I'm going home with my good wife.

MERIDIAN: What was the last thing my son said to you—before you shot him down—like a dog?

LYLE: Like a dog! You a smart nigger, ain't you?

MERIDIAN: What was the last thing he said? Did he beg you for his life?

LYLE: *That* nigger! He was too smart for that! He was too full of himself for that! He must have thought he was white. And I gave him every chance—every chance—to live!

MERIDIAN: And he refused them all.

LYLE: Do you know what that nigger said to me?
(*The light changes, so that everyone but Lyle is in silhouette. Richard appears, dressed as we last saw him, on the road outside Papa D.'s joint.*)

RICHARD: I'm ready. Here I am. You asked me if I was ready, didn't you? What's on your mind, white man?

LYLE: Boy, I always treated you with respect. I don't know what's the matter with you, or what makes you act the way you do —but you owe me an apology and I come out here tonight to get it. I mean, I ain't going away without it.

RICHARD: *I* owe *you* an apology! That's a wild idea. What am I apologizing for?

LYLE: You know, you mighty lucky to still be walking around.

RICHARD: So are you. White man.

LYLE: I'd like you to apologize for your behavior in my store that day. Now, I think I'm being pretty reasonable, ain't I?

RICHARD: You got anything to write on? I'll write you an IOU.

LYLE: Keep it up. You going to be laughing out of the other side of your mouth pretty soon.

RICHARD: Why don't you go home? And let me go home? Do we need all this shit? Can't we live without it?

LYLE: Boy, are you drunk?

RICHARD: No, I ain't drunk. I'm just tired. Tired of all this fighting. What are you trying to prove? What am *I* trying to prove?

LYLE: I'm trying to give you a break. You too dumb to take it.

RICHARD: I'm hip. You been trying to give me a break for a great, long time. But there's only one break I want. And you won't give me that.

LYLE: What kind of break do you want, boy?

RICHARD: For you to go home. And let me go home. I got things to do. I got—lots of things to do!

LYLE: I got things to do, too. I'd like to get home, too.

RICHARD: Then why are we standing here? Can't we walk? Let me walk, white man! Let me walk!

LYLE: We can walk, just as soon as we get our business settled.

RICHARD: It's settled. You a man and I'm a man. Let's walk.

LYLE: Nigger, you was born down here. Ain't you never said sir to a white man?

RICHARD: No. The only person I ever said sir to was my Daddy.

LYLE: Are you going to apologize to me?

RICHARD: No.

LYLE: Do you want to live?

RICHARD: Yes.

LYLE: Then you know what to do, then, don't you?

RICHARD: Go home. Go home.

LYLE: You facing my gun. (*Produces it*) Now, in just a minute, we can both go home.

RICHARD: You sick mother! Why can't you leave me alone? White man! I don't want nothing from you. You ain't got nothing to give me. You can't eat because none of your sad-assed chicks can cook. You can't talk because won't nobody talk to you. You can't dance because you've got nobody to dance with—don't you know I've watched you all my life? *All my life!* And I know your women, don't you think I don't— better than you!

119

*(Lyle shoots, once.)*

Why have you spent so much time trying to kill me? Why are you always trying to cut off *my* cock? You worried about it? Why?

*(Lyle shoots again.)*

Okay. Okay. Okay. Keep your old lady home, you hear? Don't let her near no nigger. She might get to like it. You might get to like it, too. Wow!

*(Richard falls.)*

Juanita! Daddy! *Mama!*

*(Singing from the church. Spot on Lyle)*

LYLE: I had to kill him then. I'm a white man! Can't nobody talk that way to *me!* I had to go and get my pick-up truck and load him in it—I had to carry him on my back—and carry him out to the high weeds. And I dumped him in the weeds, face down. And then I come on home, to my good Jo here.

JO: Come on, Lyle. We got to get on home. We got to get the little one home now.

LYLE: And I ain't sorry. I want you to know that I ain't sorry!

JO: Come on, Lyle. Come on. He's hungry. I got to feed him.

*(Jo and Lyle exit.)*

MOTHER HENRY: We got to go now, children. The children is already started to march.

LORENZO: Prayer!

MERIDIAN: You know, for us, it all began with the Bible and the gun. Maybe it will end with the Bible and the gun.

JUANITA: What did you do with the gun, Meridian?

PARNELL: You have the gun—Richard's gun?

MERIDIAN: Yes. In the pulpit. Under the Bible. Like the pilgrims of old.

*(Exits.)*

MOTHER HENRY: Come on, children.

>    (*Singing*)

>    (*Pete enters.*)

PETE (*Stammers*): Are you ready, Juanita? Shall we go now?

JUANITA: Yes.

LORENZO: Come here, Pete. Stay close to me.

>    (*They go to the church door. The singing swells.*)

PARNELL: Well.

JUANITA: Well. Yes, Lord!

PARNELL: Can I join you on the march, Juanita? Can I walk with you?

JUANITA: Well, we can walk in the same direction, Parnell. Come. Don't look like that. Let's go on on.

>    (*Exits.*)

>    (*After a moment, Parnell follows.*)


>    *Curtain*


>    **THE END**

# *note on*
# *the Author*

JAMES BALDWIN was born in New York City where he grew up and attended school, graduating from De Witt Clinton High School. His stature as both novelist and essayist has grown steadily in the years since the publication of his first novel. Mr. Baldwin has also achieved international prominence as a leader and spokesman in the civil rights movement.

Mr. Baldwin is the author of three novels, *Go Tell It on the Mountain, Giovanni's Room* and *Another Country,* and three books of essays, *Notes of a Native Son, Nobody Knows My Name* and *The Fire Next Time.* His first play, *The Amen Corner,* was produced at Howard University and his second, a dramatization of *Giovanni's Room,* at the Actors Studio workshop. His stories and essays have appeared in many magazines both here and abroad.

James Baldwin has received many literary honors. He is the winner of a Eugene F. Saxton Memorial Trust Award, a Rosenwald Fellowship, a Guggenheim Fellowship, a *Partisan Review* Fellowship and a Ford Foundation Grant-in-Aid; and he has recently been elected to the National Institute of Arts and Letters.

*Nobody Knows My Name* received a Certificate of Recognition from the National Council of Christians and Jews. Both *Nobody Knows My Name* and *The Fire Next Time* were selected by the Notable Books Council of the American Library Association and both have been included among the ten best books lists selected by the National Association of Independent Schools.